STITCH & STENCIL
Over 25 Easy Fabric-Based Projects
FOR THE HOME

This edition published by Silverdale Books,
an imprint of Bookmart Ltd, in 2000

Bookmart Ltd
Desford Road,
Enderby,
Leicester LE9 5AD

Registered Number 2372865

Produced by Eaglemoss Publications
Based on *Needlecraft Magic*
Copyright © Eaglemoss Publications Ltd 2000

Printed in Italy

ISBN 1-85605-588-4

10 9 8 7 6 5 4 3 2 1

CONTENTS

STOCKISTS AND SUPPLIERS

DMC cottons/floss:

DMC Creative World
Pullman Road
Wigston
Leicester LE18 2DY
UK

The DMC Corporation
Port Kearny
Building 10
South Kearny
New Jersey 07032
USA

DMC
51-66 Carrington Road
Marrickville
New South Wales 2204
Australia

Warnaar Trading
   Company Ltd
376 Ferry Road
PO Box 19567
Christchurch
New Zealand

S.A.T.C.
43 Somerset Road
PO Box 3868
Cape Town 8000
South Africa

Pebeo paints:

Pebeo UK
109 Solent Business Centre
Millbrook Road West
Millbrook
Southampton SO15 OHW
UK

Pebeo of America
Airport Road
PO Box 717
Swanton
VT 05488
USA

National Art
   Materials Pty Ltd
PO Box 678
Croydon
3136 Victoria
Australia

Pebeo Canada
1905 Roy Street
Sherbrooke
Quebec
Canada J1K 2X5

Liserfam Investments
   Pty Ltd
PO Box 1721
Bedfordview
2008 Johannesburg
South Africa

Lefranc et Bourgeois Textil paints:

ColArt Fine Art
   and Graphics
Whitefriars Avenue
Wealdstone
Harrow
Middlesex HA3 5RH
UK

ColArt Americas
11 Constitution Avenue
PO Box 1396
Piscataway
NJ 08855-1396
USA

Arjo Wiggins Pty Ltd
13-19 Keysborough Avenue
Keysborough
3173 Victoria
Australia

Maison 39
51 Ponsonby Road
PO Box 47184
Auckland
New Zealand

Ashley & Radmore
PO Box 57324
Johannesburg 2137
South Africa

ACKNOWLEDGMENTS

Photographs: Edward Allwright, Paul Bricknell, Alan Duns, Christine Hanscombe,
Gloria Nicol, Lizzie Orme, Steven Pam, Russell Sadur, Lucinda Symons,
Adrian Taylor, Shona Wood

Illustrations: Terry Evans, Sally Holmes, Coral Mula

Stencils by Tessa Brown. Stitches by Sheila Coulson

CHAIRS

STYLE AND PRACTICALITY JOIN HANDS WITH
CHAIR PROTECTORS THAT ENHANCE THE LOOK
OF YOUR FAVOURITE
ARMCHAIR.

CHAIR BACK COVERS

Tradition takes on a modern twist with coordinating panels and stencilled chairs.

COLOUR KEY

COLOURS	SKEINS
■ 3809 Dark aqua	2
■ 3810 Aqua	1

PAINT COLOUR GUIDE

For the chairs: mix Opaque Duck Blue paint with a dab of White to make mid aqua.

This smartly tailored chair back cover – or antimacassar – features a row of chairs stencilled in cool aqua and embellished with outline stitches and French knots.

The antimacassar is made in a trio of cotton furnishing fabrics in shades of green and cream. The instructions are for a 21in (53cm) wide cover. If you want a narrower cover, stencil fewer chairs. For details on making antimacassars, refer to page 55.

Preparing the stencil

You will need all the cutouts on the chair stencil (below), so mask off nearby cutouts as you work. In the diagram the chairs are numbered **1-3** for easy identification as you work.

Cutting out

Make a paper pattern for the antimacassar 21in (53cm) wide and a suitable length for your chair, then measure up for the straps. For details see page 55. Cut out the pieces, referring to the instructions below. *From the sea green fabric*: cut the lining and two straps; cut the main piece 7½in (19cm) shorter than the lining. *From the cream fabric*: cut a 22¼ x 6in (56 x 15cm) contrast strip. *From the eau de nil fabric*: cut one 22¼ x 4in (56 x 10cm) piece for the bottom strip.

Preparing to stencil

Fold the cream strip in half widthwise and press the fold lightly with an iron. Press a crease 1in (2.5cm) from one long edge. Unfold the fabric and tape it to the work surface with the short edges at the sides and the long crease close to you.

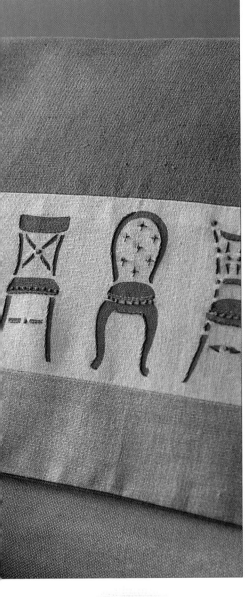

STENCILLING THE CHAIRS

1 Centre the middle chair cutout (cutout **2**) on the centre foldline with the feet sitting on the horizontal foldline. Stencil the chair with mid aqua paint.

2 Move the stencil a little way to the right and position the right-hand chair cutout (cutout **3**) 1in (2.5cm) from the middle chair, with its feet on the foldline. Stencil it with mid aqua paint. ▲

3 Move the stencil over to the left and position the left-hand chair cutout (cutout **1**) 1in (2.5cm) from the stencilled middle chair. Stencil it with mid aqua paint.

4 Continue in this way to stencil two more chairs to the left and two to the right, spacing them 1in (2.5cm) apart. Make sure the feet are on the horizontal crease. Allow the paint to dry and fix it with a hot iron. ▼

EMBROIDERING THE CHAIRS

Mount the fabric in the hoop and using three strands of cotton (floss) unless stated otherwise, add detail with stem and straight stitch and French knots (see below).

Making up

Assemble the antimacassar following the instructions on page 55; use the stencilled chair strip as the contrast strip.

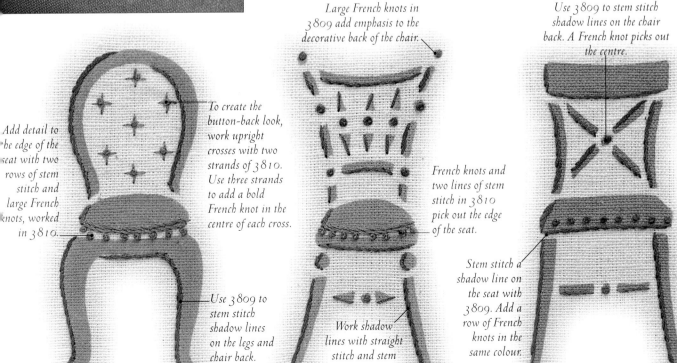

Add detail to the edge of the seat with two rows of stem stitch and large French knots, worked in 3810.

To create the button-back look, work upright crosses with two strands of 3810. Use three strands to add a bold French knot in the centre of each cross.

Use 3809 to stem stitch shadow lines on the legs and chair back.

Large French knots in 3809 add emphasis to the decorative back of the chair.

French knots and two lines of stem stitch in 3810 pick out the edge of the seat.

Work shadow lines with straight stitch and stem stitch, using 3809.

Use 3809 to stem stitch shadow lines on the chair back. A French knot picks out the centre.

Stem stitch a shadow line on the seat with 3809. Add a row of French knots in the same colour.

CHAIR ARMCAPS

Rows of chairs stencilled and decoratively stitched along the front and side edges of these smart armcaps coordinate perfectly with the stylish chair back cover.

YOU WILL NEED

For a pair of armcaps:

❁ ⅞yd (80cm) of eau de nil Indian canvas

❁ Sea green Indian canvas for the piping

❁ Piping cord

❁ Stencilling and stitching materials and equipment listed on page 6

Preparing the stencil

For the armcaps, you will be using the complete chair stencil, so mask off any nearby cut-outs as you work.

Emphasize the shapes on the chair back with straight stitches and French knots worked with 3809.

To pick out the front of the chair seat, work a double row of stem stitch, and a row of knobbly French knots in 3810.

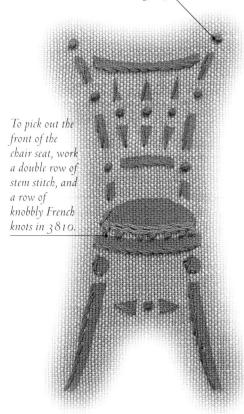

STENCILLING THE ARMCAP

1 *From the eau de nil fabric:* cut out the armcaps, as on page 55. Press a crease 2in (5cm) from one short edge of each piece. Place this edge nearest you on the work surface.

2 On the front pieces, use mid aqua to stencil two chairs with their feet on the creased line. Space them 1in (2.5cm) apart, centred across the width of the fabric. ➤

3 On the main pieces, stencil a row of four chairs sitting on the crease; centre them across the width, spaced 1in (2.5cm) apart as before. Allow the paint to dry and fix it with a hot iron.

STITCHING THE ARMCAP

Embroider the stencilled chairs on the armcaps in the same way as the stencilled chairs on the antimacassar. Refer to the stitch details (left) and the instructions and stitch details on page 7.

Cover the piping cord with the sea green fabric, then stitch the piping round the top and side edges of the front pieces. Make up the covers referring to page 55.

PUSSY WILLOW

SLENDER TWIGS CLOTHED IN PLUMP
FURRY BUDS ARE DEPICTED IN
ELEGANT DESIGNS FOR
THE HOME.

YOU WILL NEED

* Brown curtain
* ½yd (40cm) of brown fabric for the cushion
* Beige cotton fabric for the pussy willow panels
* Stencil and stencil brush
* Pebeo fabric paints in Chamois, Pearl Pearl and Velvet Brown
* Kitchen paper and wallpaper lining paper
* Masking tape
* DMC stranded cottons/ floss and Anchor Marlitt threads as listed in the colour key
* Embroidery needles, size 5 and 7
* Embroidery hoop
* Cushion pad/insert, 17¾ x 13¾in (45 x 35cm)

COLOUR KEY

COLOURS	SKEINS
DMC stranded cottons/floss	
Ecru	3
838 Black coffee	1
839 Dark coffee	2
Anchor Marlitt threads	
845 Pale grey	1
870 Dark grey	1
1034 Ecru	1

PAINT COLOUR GUIDE

For the twigs: use Chamois.

For the large buds: use Pearl Pearl.

For the small buds: use Velvet Brown.

PUSSY WILLOW CROSSES

Beautiful pussy willow panels, stencilled and embroidered in gleaming threads, add understated elegance to a matching curtain and cushion.

Preparing the stencil

The diagram (right) shows the pussy willow stencil. You will be using all the cutouts. You will be stencilling the twigs first. Before you start to stencil, mask off any cutouts close to the one you are using.

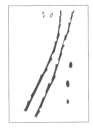

Preparing the fabric

For the cushion: cut a 13¾ x 6¾in (38 x 17cm) piece of beige fabric. *For the curtain*: measure from the base of the heading tape or tabs and add on 1¼in (3cm); cut a 6¾in (17cm) wide strip to this length. Tape the fabric pieces on to the prepared work surface with the long edges at the sides.

STENCILLING THE PUSSY WILLOW

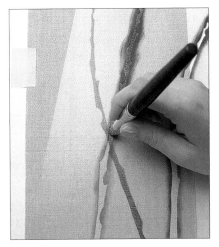

1 Centre a twig cutout on the beige cushion fabric, and pivot it slightly. Dry brush it using Chamois. Dry brush the second twig cutout to form a cross. ▲

2 Position the larger bud cutouts in the curved niches in the stencilled twigs and stencil them with Pearl Pearl paint. ▲

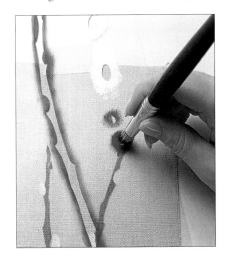

3 Stencil the tiny buds at the tips of the twigs with Velvet Brown paint. When all the paints are dry, fix them with a hot iron. ▲

4 Follow steps 1-3 to stencil crossed twigs down the length of the curtain strip. Position the first cross 2¼in (6cm) from the bottom of the strip, and space the pairs about 2¼in (6cm) apart.

EMBROIDERING

Pad the buds with two layers of satin stitch: use the size 5 needle and four strands of ecru stranded cotton (floss). Refer to the details (right) to complete the embroidery using the size 7 needle.

Making up the cushion

From the brown fabric: cut a 15 x 3½in (38 x 9cm) strip and a 15 x 11¼in (38 x 28cm) piece. Taking ⅝in (1.5cm) seam allowances, stitch the brown strip to the left-hand side of the pussy willow panel, and the brown rectangle to the right-hand side. Finish the cushion as shown on page 59.

Making up the curtain

Press in ⅝in (1.5cm) all around the curtain panel. Pin it on to the curtain, with the lower edges level and the outer edge level with the leading edge of the curtain. Stitch it in place by hand or machine.

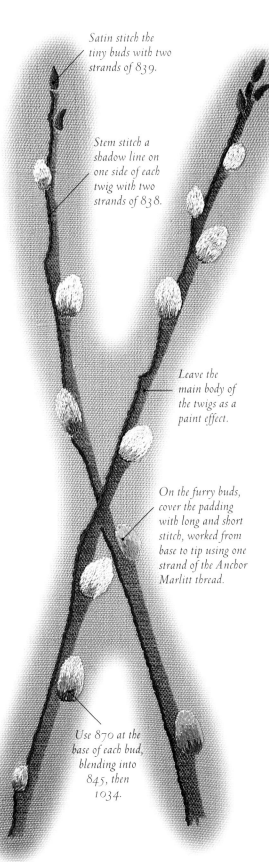

Satin stitch the tiny buds with two strands of 839.

Stem stitch a shadow line on one side of each twig with two strands of 838.

Leave the main body of the twigs as a paint effect.

On the furry buds, cover the padding with long and short stitch, worked from base to tip using one strand of the Anchor Marlitt thread.

Use 870 at the base of each bud, blending into 845, then 1034.

SQUARE CUSHION

A row of pussy willow twigs adorns this smart cushion cover, designed to coordinate with the curtain and cushion set. To add variety, the twigs are fully stitched and the cover has a mitred border.

YOU WILL NEED

* ⅝yd (50cm) beige cotton fabric
* Stitching and stencilling equipment as listed on page 10
* Embroidery threads listed on page 10, plus one skein of DMC stranded cotton/ floss 840
* Cushion pad/insert, 17½in (45cm) square

STENCILLING

Cut a 19¾in (50cm) square of fabric. Starting in the centre of the fabric square, stencil a row of parallel twigs, spaced about 1½in (4cm) apart. Stencil them as for the cushion and curtain on the previous page, but flip the stencil so some twigs bend the other way.

EMBROIDERING

Refer to the stitch details (right). To pad the large buds, use four strands of the ecru stranded cotton (floss) and the size 5 needle to work two layers of satin stitch.

Change to the number 7 needle. Using one strand of Anchor Marlitt thread, cover the buds with long and short stitch, blending dark grey at the base into light grey, then ecru.

Using two strands of DMC stranded cotton (floss), satin stitch the twigs using 839. Work a stem stitch shadow line in 838 on one side of each twig, and satin stitch the tiny buds at the tips in 840.

MITRED SINGLE BORDERS

Attaching the border strips

1 Add twice the seam allowance to the width of the border to get A. Measure one edge of the centre panel and add on twice the width of the border plus an extra 1in (2.5cm) for mitring to get B. Cut out two strips A by B.

2 Mark the centre of one border strip and the centre of one of the appropriate sides of the panel. Centre the strip on the panel side, with the right sides together, raw edges matching; pin.

3 Stitch the border strip, beginning and ending ¼in (6mm) in from the finished corner position on the panel; backstitch at each end of the stitchline. Repeat with the other border strip.

4 Press the border strips to the right side, away from the panel.

Machine-stitched mitres

1 Place the panel wrong side up. At one corner, fold back each border strip at a 45° angle, making sure that the folds touch, and press.

2 Pin the borders together along the pressed folds. Machine stitch along the foldline, working from the outside edge towards the panel.

3 Trim the seam allowances and press them open. Repeat to stitch mitres at the other three corners.

Making up the cushion

Trim the twig panel to 13¾in (35cm) square. Add a single mitred border with a finished width of 2½in (6.5cm) (see above). Finish the cushion with an overlapped back, referring to page 59.

Satin stitch the small buds with two strands of 840.

A double layer of satin stitch padding gives the furry buds a plump, raised finish.

For a neat finish, fill the twigs with slanted satin stitch.

Cover the padding on the buds with long and short stitch and gleaming Anchor Marlitt threads.

Work vertically from the base to the tip, starting with the darkest colour.

A stem stitched shadow line adds shape to the twig.

SPIRALS

APPLIQUED AND STENCILLED SPIRALS
COMBINE WITH CURVY SCALLOPED EDGES
TO CREATE FURNISHINGS WITH A SOFT
YET MODERN TOUCH.

SPIRAL CUSHION

Felt does not fray and is magically simple to use
to create this stylish cushion cover.

YOU WILL NEED

- ¾yd (60cm) of 36in (90cm) wide lilac felt
- ⅝yd (50cm) of 36in (90cm) wide lime green felt
- ⅝yd (50cm) of 36in (90cm) wide pale blue felt
- Spiral stencil
- Pencil and ruler
- Tracing paper
- Thin white card
- Craft knife
- Sharp pointed scissors
- Pins
- Spray mount
- DMC stranded cottons/ floss as listed in colour key
- Embroidery needles, sizes 5 and 7
- Sewing thread to match the lilac felt
- 13¾in (35cm) square cushion pad/insert

COLOUR KEY

COLOURS	SKEINS
553 Violet	1
3819 Lime moss	1

Preparing the stencil
The diagram (above) shows the spiral stencil. For the cushion, you will be using the spiral cutout as a positioning guide.

Layers of coloured felt joined with bold stitching form the central panel of the cushion cover. The scalloped edge of the pale blue felt is cut using the template on page 75; the spiral cutout, also on page 75, is used as a positioning guide for the appliqué spirals.

Use the colours suggested here or create your own eyecatching colour combination to suit your room scheme. You can buy felt by the yard (metre) from specialist craft shops and mail order companies, and some department stores. Remember to ask before you buy whether the felt is washable or dry-clean only.

The cushion cover measures 13¾in (35cm) square. The felt quantities given here include enough to make the matching tieback (see page 16).

Making the scallop template

Trace the scallop template on page 75. Spray mount the tracing on to the thin white card and cut it out with scissors or a craft knife. Spray mount the back of the card templat and leave to dry.

Cutting out

From lilac felt: cut a 6¼in (16cm) square for the spiral panel, a 15in (38cm) square for the front and two 15 x 10in (38 x 25cm) pieces for the back.

From lime green felt: cut an 8in (20cm) square panel and four 11 x ¼in (28cm x 6mm) strips for the spirals.

From pale blue felt: cut one 12in (30cm) square for the scalloped panel.

MAKING THE PANELS

1 In the centre of the blue felt square, draw a 7¼in (18.5cm) square. Mark the centre of each edge of the drawn square. Mark the centre of the straight edge of the scallop template.

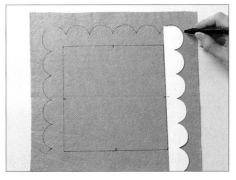

2 Place the straight edge of the template on one edge of the drawn square with the scallops facing out and the centre marks matching. Draw around the scallops. Repeat on each edge, rounding off the corner scallops. Use the sharp pointed scissors to cut out the panel along the drawn scalloped line. Use the drawn side as the wrong side. ◄

3 Use the pins to divide the smaller lilac felt square into quarters. Centre the spiral cutout in one quarter and draw carefully along the centre of the spiral. Repeat in each quarter. ◄

4 Place the end of a lime green felt strip at the outer end of one marked spiral. With four strands of violet cotton (floss) and the size 7 embroidery needle, stitch the strip over the spiral with large running stitches. Repeat on the other three spirals.

For a smooth curve, stretch the felt strips slightly as you work around the spirals.

STITCHING THE CUSHION COVER

Centre the lilac spiral panel on the lime green panel and pin it in place. Work French knots all around the edge of the lilac square through both layers; use six strands of lime moss and the size 5 needle. Place the knots ⅝in (1.5cm) apart, with a knot in each corner.

Centre the lime green panel on the scalloped blue panel, and the blue panel on the large square lilac panel; stitch through all three layers with bold running stitches; use four strands of violet and place the stitches ¼in (6mm) in from the edge of the lime green panel.

Making up

Taking ⅝in (1.5cm) seam allowances, make up the cushion cover as on page 59.

Make sure the running stitches and the French knots are evenly spaced.

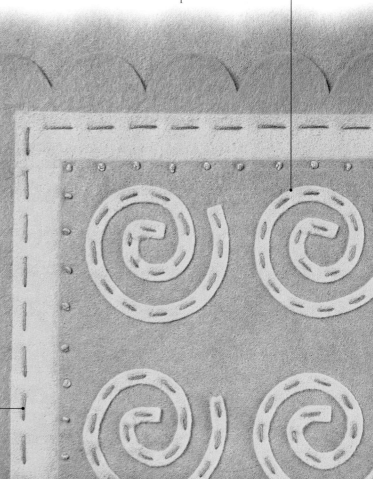

CURTAIN TIEBACK

This spiral felt tieback makes a bold statement against a plain curtain. It matches the cushion, but the spirals are stencilled with purple fabric paint to vary the look.

PREPARING THE PANELS

1 Cut a 23 x 3⅜in (58 x 8.5cm) strip of lilac felt. Stencil six purple spirals along the centre, ending ¾in (2cm) from each end. Allow the paint to dry and fix it with a warm iron. ▶

2 Cut a 27½ x 8in (70 x 20cm) strip of blue felt. In the centre, draw a 24 x 4in (61 x 10cm) rectangle. Mark the centre of each edge.

3 Starting at the centre of each edge, draw the scallops as for the cushion on page 15; move the template along as required. Cut along the marked lines.

Work even running stitches along the centre of the stencilled spirals.

STITCHING

Using four strands of lime moss and the size 7 needle, work running stitches along the centre of each spiral.

Cut a 24 x 4¾in (61 x 12cm) panel of lime green felt. Referring to the cushion cover on page 15, stitch the lilac spiral panel to the lime green panel with lime moss French knots, then stitch the lime green panel to the blue scalloped panel with violet running stitches.

Making up

Cut a 23¾ x 4¼in (60 x 11.5cm) piece of pelmet Vilene and centre it on the wrong side of the tieback, covering all the stitching. Pin then slipstitch in place. Stitch a brass ring at each end of the tieback on the wrong side.

GEOMETRIC BLOCKS

TAKE SIMPLICITY TO ITS LIMITS WITH
CHUNKY COLOUR BLOCKS AND
BOLD STITCHES TO CREATE A
CONTEMPORARY MOOD.

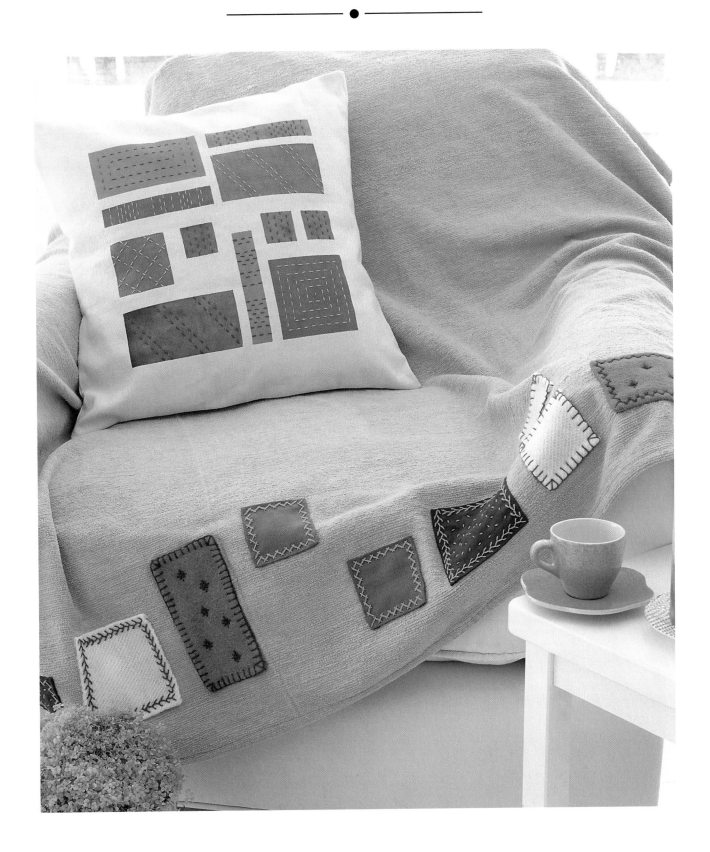

APPLIQUE BLOCK THROW

Making an original designer throw couldn't be easier – all it takes is a few bright fabric blocks and bold embroidery stitches.

Wool patches in four colours are arranged in a random order along one edge of a plain blanket and stitched in place with three basic stitches. You can stitch blocks along just one edge of the blanket, as shown here, or continue the design round two, three or all four sides of the blanket, depending on how it will be displayed.

Using the stencil

The diagram (right) shows the geometric block stencil. You will be using the large rectangle and  the two largest squares as templates for cutting the patches, so there is no need to do any masking off.

WORKING THE APPLIQUE

1 On the paper, draw around the inside of the large rectangle cutout several times. Repeat with the two largest square cutouts. Cut out the shapes.

2 To plan your block design, place the paper shapes in a random row 2¼in (6cm) from the edge of the blanket. When you are happy with the arrangement, pin them in place. Note which colour to use on each paper shape. ▲

3 Use the air-erasable fabric marker to draw around the inside of each of the two cutouts on to the four patch fabrics. Leave a 1½in (4cm) gap between the shapes and make sure that you draw the correct number of shapes on to the appropriate coloured fabric.

4 Cut out each shape ⅜in (1cm) outside the drawn lines. Turn in the edges of each patch along the drawn lines and tack the turnings in place. ▲

5 One at a time, pin the patches in position on the blanket; remove the appropriate paper shape first. Using two strands of wool in the colours of your choice, refer to the stitch details (right) to stitch them in place.

Straight lines of feather stitch soften the shape of square blocks.

Herringbone stitch worked just inside the edges creates a decorative zigzag effect.

Scatter seeding stitches at random over the darker squares.

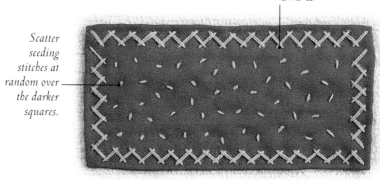

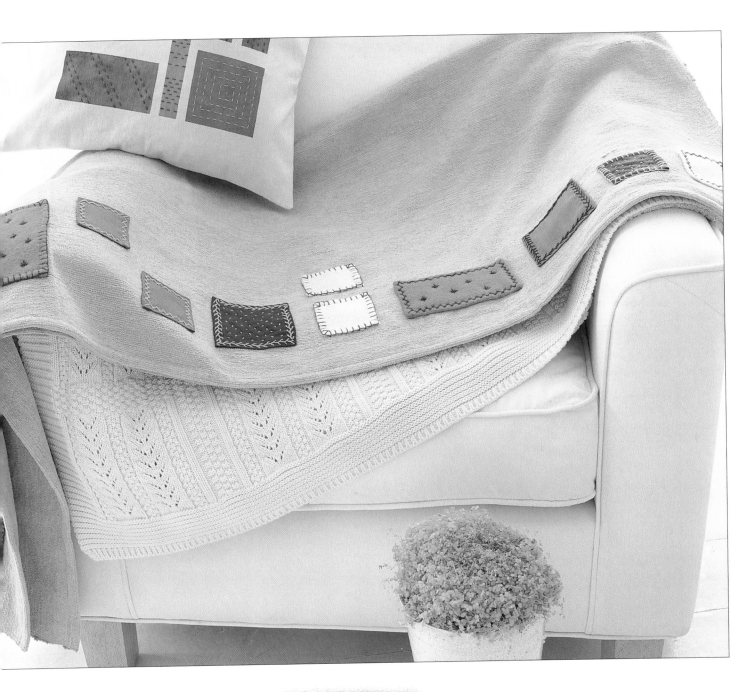

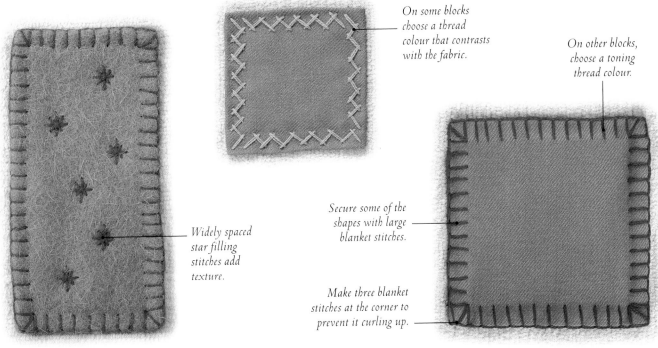

On some blocks
choose a thread
colour that contrasts
with the fabric.

On other blocks,
choose a toning
thread colour.

Widely spaced
star filling
stitches add
texture.

Secure some of the
shapes with large
blanket stitches.

Make three blanket
stitches at the corner to
prevent it curling up.

BLOCK CUSHION

YOU WILL NEED

* ⅝yd (50cm) of cream furnishing cotton
* Geometric block stencil and stencil brush
* Pebeo fabric paints in Opaque Light Green, Transparent Light Green, Transparent Turquoise and Transparent Fluorescent Blue
* Masking tape
* Kitchen paper and wallpaper lining paper
* Spray mount
* Paper and pencil
* Tacking thread and needle
* DMC stranded cottons/floss as listed in the colour key
* Embroidery needle, size 7
* Embroidery hoop
* Cushion pad/insert, 17¾in (45cm) square

COLOUR KEY

COLOURS	SKEINS
704 Pale spring green	1
824 Rich blue	1
996 Mid turquoise	1

STENCILLING THE BLOCKS

Preparing the stencil

You need all the geometric block cutouts for the cushion. Before you begin, spray mount the back of the stencil and allow it to dry. As you work, mask off any cutouts close to the one you are using.

Preparing the fabric

Cut a 19in (48cm) square of cream fabric for the cushion cover front. Tack an 11½in (29cm) square in the centre to mark the design area.

1 On the paper, use the stencil to draw one large, one medium and three small squares, then draw three large and three narrow rectangles. Cut them out and tape them on the fabric in the tacked square in a pleasing design with the outer edges on the tacked lines. ▲

STITCHING

Remove the tacking threads and mount the stencilled fabric in the embroidery hoop. Use two strands of cotton (floss) to decorate the blocks with bold running stitches; use a different cotton (floss)

2 Align the appropriate cutout over the top left-hand paper block. Remove the paper and stencil the block with one paint colour – use neat paint. Repeat to stencil the rest of the blocks, alternating the colours. When complete, leave the paint to dry and fix it with a hot iron. ▲

colour for each paint colour and refer to the picture (above) for design ideas.

Make up a 17¾in (45cm) square cushion cover with an overlapped back, referring to page 59.

CROWNS AND CORONETS

GLITTERING CROWNS AND CORONETS ADD
HERALDIC SPLENDOUR TO THE DINING ROOM.
USE YOUR STENCILS TO CREATE A SUMPTUOUS TABLE RUNNER
AND CHAIR SEAT COVER.

REGAL TABLE RUNNER

Dine in opulence at a table set with this distinctive runner. The crowns are embellished with metallic threads, beads and sequins.

YOU WILL NEED

For the runner:

* ¼yd (20cm) red Dupion silk fabric
* ½yd (40cm) of red velvet, 52in (130cm) wide
* Red lining fabric, 63 x 14½in (1.6m x 37cm)
* ⅞yd (70cm) of gold fringing
* Lefranc et Bourgeois Textil Paint in Black
* Stencil and stencil brush
* White saucer
* Masking tape
* Wallpaper lining paper
* Pencil and ruler
* One skein of DMC metallic gold stranded cotton/floss 5282
* One skein of Kreinik Japan thread #7
* DMC metallic gold thread ART D280
* Embroidery needle, size 8
* Beading needle
* Needle threader (optional)
* Embroidery hoop
* Scissors
* Pack of 8mm gold sequins
* Pack of 5mm gold sequins
* Vial of gold seed beads
* Gold bugle beads

Preparing the stencil

The diagram below shows the crowns and coronets stencil. For the runner you need all the cutouts – the three crown motifs and the small Maltese cross – shown here in black.

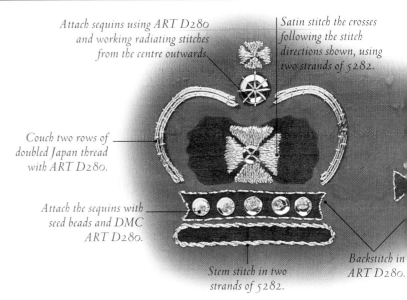

Attach sequins using ART D280 and working radiating stitches from the centre outwards.

Satin stitch the crosses following the stitch directions shown, using two strands of 5282.

Couch two rows of doubled Japan thread with ART D280.

Attach the sequins with seed beads and DMC ART D280.

Stem stitch in two strands of 5282.

Backstitch in ART D280.

POSITIONING THE DESIGN

The three crowns, with Maltese crosses between, are stencilled in a row on to silk panels. The panels are embroidered and then stitched on to velvet to make a firm, plush runner. To prepare the panels, cut the silk into two 14½in x 6¾in (37 x 17cm) rectangles.

To position the motifs, fold each rectangle in half widthwise and press the creases. Unfold and press two vertical creases, 4in (10cm) each side of the central one. Unfold, then press a horizontal crease 2⅛in (5½cm) from the long lower edge.

STENCILLING THE RUNNER

1 Position the fleur de lys crown cutout on one fabric rectangle so that it is centred over the central vertical crease. Position the base on the horizontal crease. Stencil the crown in black paint using a dry brush.

2 Centre the round crown over the left-hand vertical crease and stencil in black. Repeat to stencil the pointed crown over the right-hand crease. ▼

3 Stencil a small Maltese cross between two crown motifs, with its base ⅜in (1cm) above the horizontal crease. Using a pencil and ruler, mark the position of the horizontal crease on the stencil. Using this mark as a positioning guide, stencil three more crosses. Repeat steps 1-3 to stencil the second silk panel for the opposite end of the runner. Leave the paint to dry, then fix it with an iron. ▼

MAKING UP THE RUNNER

Trim the velvet to measure 52 x 14½in (130cm x 37cm). Measure and cut off a 14½ x 7½in (37 x 19cm) piece from each end. Right sides together, with the crowns pointing towards the seam, stitch an embroidered band to each end of the main velvet rectangle. Stitch a velvet strip to each end of the runner. Lay a length of fringing across each end

of the velvet, so the fringes point towards the centre of the runner and the fringing band lies inside the seam allowance. Right sides together, place the lining over the velvet and stitch around outer edge, taking ⅝in (1.5cm) seams, stitching in fringing and leaving a small opening for turning. Turn through to the right side and press. Slipstitch the gap closed.

STITCHING GUIDE

Refer to the stitch details (below) to bead and embroider the motifs – each one is worked slightly differently. To prevent metallic threads from splitting and fraying as you stitch, work with lengths of no longer than 8in (20cm).

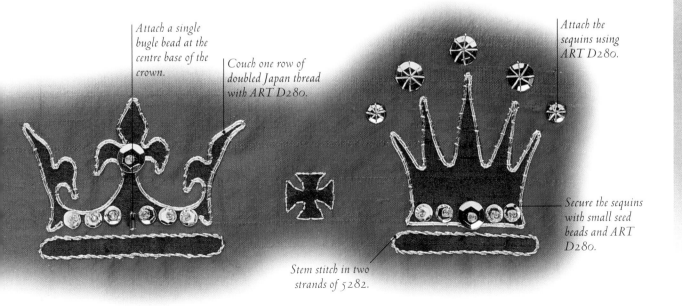

Attach a single bugle bead at the centre base of the crown.

Couch one row of doubled Japan thread with ART D280.

Attach the sequins using ART D280.

Secure the sequins with small seed beads and ART D280.

Stem stitch in two strands of 5282.

CROWN SEAT COVER

YOU WILL NEED

For the seat cover:

❋ Red Dupion silk fabric

❋ Stencil paint and equipment as listed on page 22

❋ One skein each of DMC stranded cotton/floss 3820 gold and 834 pale gold

❋ Embroidery needle, size 8

Decorate a drop-in seat cover with the crown motifs. Where and how you position the motifs depends on the size of your chair seat. Make a tracing of your chair seat and use this to plan the position of the motifs. You could also use these embroidered crowns to make a plush scatter cushion cover or even an exotic tablecloth. Follow the instructions on the previous page to stencil the motifs in black.

STITCHING GUIDE

Mount the fabric in an embroidery hoop and embroider each motif individually, referring to the stitch details (right). Unless otherwise stated, use one strand each of 834 and 3820 together in the needle throughout. Cover the seat pad, following the instructions on page 56.

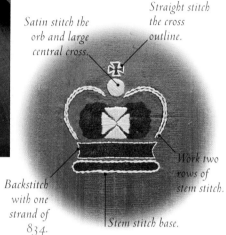

Satin stitch the orb and large central cross.

Straight stitch the cross outline.

Backstitch with one strand of 834.

Work two rows of stem stitch.

Stem stitch base.

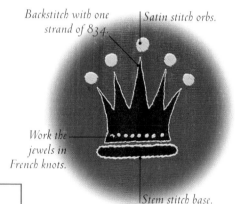

Backstitch with one strand of 834.

Satin stitch orbs.

Work the jewels in French knots.

Stem stitch base.

BRIGHT IDEAS

HERALDIC HOLDBACK

Use the large Maltese cross to make a fabulous curtain holdback. You can buy holdback kits in most department stores — you simply add the fabric of your choice. This holdback uses red silk, stencilled with a large black cross. The outer edges of the cross are outlined with couched double Japan thread. The inner line is backstitched with gold stranded cotton (floss). Four bugle beads, and sequins secured with tiny beads complete the design.

Add French knots for the jewels.

Backstitch in one strand of 834.

Stem stitch base.

PANSIES

VELVETY PANSIES STENCILLED AND
STITCHED ON SHEER TABLE LINEN
CREATE A PRETTY SETTING FOR
SUMMER DINING.

YOU WILL NEED

❈ White organza tablecloth

❈ Pansy stencil and stencil brush

❈ Fine watercolour brush

❈ Pebeo fabric paints in Green Gold, White, Parma Violet, Fawn, Ultramarine Blue, and Red Ochre

❈ Masking tape and spray mount

❈ Kitchen paper and wallpaper lining paper

❈ DMC stranded cottons/floss and rayon threads as listed in the colour key

❈ Embroidery needle, size 8

COLOUR KEY

COLOURS	SKEINS
Stranded cottons/floss	
745 Pale buttercup	I
972 Sunshine yellow	I
3346 Mid hunter green	I
Rayon thread	
30550 Dark violet	I
30554 Pale violet	I
30744 Mid buttercup	I

PAINT COLOUR GUIDE

For the leaves and stems: mix Green Gold with a little White to make mid green.

For the mid purple pansy: mix Parma Violet with a little White to make mid purple.

For the light purple pansy and bud: mix White with a little Parma Violet to make light purple.

For the gold pansy: mix White with a little Fawn to make golden yellow.

For the flower centres and shading on the petals: use the paints straight from the pots.

MID SUMMER TABLE

Lifesize posies of stencilled pansies highlighted with a little embroidery bloom among the place settings on an organza tablecloth.

The posies are stencilled in four paint colours, then more paint is applied with delicate brush strokes to add depth to the petals and the bright yellow centres are picked out with dainty stitching.

On the tablecloth shown here, the pansies are placed within squares formed by the grid on a ready-made organza tablecloth. On a plain cloth, arrange them at measured intervals or scatter them at random.

Preparing the stencil

The diagram (below) shows the pansy stencil. You will be using the complete design, so mask off any other nearby cut-outs before you start, then spray mount the back of the stencil and leave it to dry.

Preparing the tablecloth

Lay the cloth on the table and decide where you want to position the pansy posies. Use pins to mark the bottom of the stalk on each posy.

STENCILLING THE PANSIES

1 Mask the stencil to expose the leaves, stems and calyx on the bud. Place the stencil in the first pin mark and remove the pin. Stencil the cutouts with mid green paint. Repeat to stencil at each marked position.

2 Remask the stencil to reveal the purple pansies and bud. Aligning the cutout on each posy, stencil the bud and left-hand pansy with light purple and the right-hand pansy with mid purple. Remask the stencil to reveal the centre pansy and stencil it with golden yellow on each posy.

3 Use the watercolour brush to make light brush strokes on the lower petals of each flower. Use Ultramarine Blue on the mid purple pansy, Parma Violet on the light purple pansy and Red Ochre on the golden yellow pansy. Fix the paint with a warm iron.

EMBROIDERING THE PANSIES

Using the stitch details for reference, work stem stitch outlines to highlight some petals, then embroider the flower centres and stems. Use single strands of thread (floss) for the flowers and two strands for the stems.

Fill the flower centres with satin stitch using a single strand of cotton (floss) 972. Then surround the centre with two long bullion knots in cotton 745, couching each knot down in the centre to hold it in place.

Work stem stitch outlines on the dark purple petals with 30550, and on the light purple flower with 30554.

Fill the two long stems with slanted satin stitch using two strands of cotton (floss) 3346.

Pick out the three lower petals on the yellow pansy with 30744 and stem stitch.

BRIGHT IDEAS

PLACE CARDS

Personalized pansy place cards make a pretty finishing touch for the pansy table. For each place card, cut or tear a 5⅛ x 4in (13 x 10cm) piece of white card and fold it in half widthwise. On white organza, stencil a single flower head and cut it out ⅛in (3mm) outside the stencilled petals. Attach the flower with a gold sequin secured with a small gold bead.

NAPKIN RINGS

For six napkin rings you will need ¼yd (20cm) of organza, some heavyweight iron-on interfacing, stencilling materials and equipment as listed on page 26, the DMC stranded cottons (floss) and rayon threads listed in the colour key, and white sewing thread.

COLOUR KEY

COLOURS	SKEINS
Stranded cottons/floss	
Ecru	1
208 Dark lavender	1
210 Mid lavender	1
550 Dark violet	1
743 Buttercup	1
745 Pale buttercup	1
972 Sunshine yellow	1
Rayon threads	
30550 Dark violet	1
30744 Mid buttercup	1

Preparing the stencil
Mask off the stencil to isolate a single flower head, spray mount the back of the stencil and leave it to dry.

Cutting out
Cut a paper pattern for a plain napkin ring 6¾ x 3in (17 x 8cm) which allows ⅜in (1cm) for seams. Use the pattern to cut two organza pieces for each ring.

Making the napkin rings
For each napkin ring, bond the interfacing to the wrong side of one piece. Stitch right sides together on the long edges, leaving ⅜in (1cm) at both ends. Turn to the right side and press. Stencil and stitch the pansies at this stage. Then to finish off, place the short raw edges of the interfaced piece together and stitch. Finger press

the seam allowances open and tuck them inside. Turn the unstitched seam allowances to the inside and pin them to hold. Slipstitch the folded edges together.

STENCILLING

Mask off the stencil to reveal the single flower, then mask off the centre. Centre the flower on one organza rectangle. Stencil the petals with mid or light purple or golden yellow paint.

STITCHING

Referring to the details for colours and stitches, and using single strands of thread throughout, fill the pansy heads completely with long and short stitch shading, and fill the centres with satin stitch and bullion knots.

Fill the small back petal with satin stitch and 972. Use the same thread to fill the larger back petal with long and short stitch, blending into 30744 towards the centre.

On the back petals, blend cotton thread (floss) 550 at the outer edges into rayon thread 30550 towards the centre.

Shade the front purple petals with long and short stitch, working from the outer edges and radiating the stitches towards the centre. Blend 210 into 208, and finally work in 30550 at the base of the petals.

Satin stitch the flower centres with 972, then work a bullion knot on each side of the centre using 743, couching them down to hold them in place.

Fill the front yellow pansy petals with long and short stitch using 30744. Work from the outer edges of the petals inwards, radiating the stitches towards the centre. Blend in black at the centre of each petal.

Bright Hearts

Colourful fabric and stencilled hearts,
embellished with bold embroidery,
make bright decorations
for folk art kitchens.

CAFE CURTAIN

Perfect for disguising a dull outlook, this heart appliqué curtain adds a colourful flash of folk-art fun.

The café curtain has a contrasting heart border along the bottom edge, echoed by a narrower, plain border at the top. It's made up like a simple tab curtain with a couple of decorative variations – it is attached to the curtain pole by ties instead of tabs, and the top border is created by turning the facing to the front, instead of the back.

Before you start, measure up your window, as on page 58.

YOU WILL NEED

❋ Lightweight cotton fabric in lime green for the main curtain

❋ Royal blue cotton fabric for the borders and ties

❋ ⅛yd (10cm) each of three contrasting cotton fabrics for the heart appliqué

❋ Heart stencil

❋ Sharp, hard (H) pencil

❋ Bondaweb/WonderUnder

❋ DMC stranded cottons/floss as listed in colour key

❋ Embroidery needle, size 7

❋ Sewing threads to match the two main fabrics

COLOUR KEY

COLOURS	SKEINS
321 Red	1
702 Green	1
741 Orange	1
958 Aqua	1

Cutting out

From the lime green fabric: cut the curtain to the required width but 3¾in (9.5cm) shorter than the required finished length.

From the royal blue fabric: cut an 11¼in (28cm) band the width of the curtain for the bottom border; one 4in (10cm) strip the width of the curtain for the top border; and one 17 x 2in (43 x 5cm) strip for each tie.

Preparing the stencil

The diagram (right) shows the heart stencil. You will be using the heart cutout shown in colour as a template.

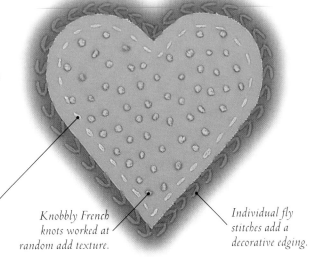

Running stitches, worked inside the edge of the appliqué hearts, help to secure them in place.

Knobbly French knots worked at random add texture.

Individual fly stitches add a decorative edging.

PREPARING THE HEARTS

1 Calculate the number of hearts you need, spaced 1⅜in (3.5cm) apart across the bottom border. Using the heart cutout as a template, draw that number of hearts on to the paper side of the Bondaweb (WonderUnder). Cut them out roughly and fuse to the wrong side of the fabrics. Then cut them out accurately. ▲

2 Press a crease 5in (12.5cm) below one long edge of the bottom border strip. Fuse the hearts on to the narrower section with the pointed tips on the creased line, spacing them 1⅜in (3.5cm) apart and alternating the fabric colours. ▲

EMBROIDERING THE HEARTS

Refer to the stitch details (below) and use three strands of cotton (floss) throughout. Work running stitch inside the edge of each heart. Work fly, chain or whipped running stitch round the outside, and fill the centre with large French knots or radiating straight stitches.

Making up the curtain

With right sides together, stitch the heart panel to the bottom edge of the curtain. Refer to page 58 to hem the sides and base, but at the base, turn in ⅝in (1.5cm), then 5in (12.5cm).

Fold the ties in half lengthwise, and stitch all around leaving a gap to turn through; turn out, press and slipstitch the gap closed.

Finish the curtain according to the instructions on page 58 but omit the interfacing and sandwich the ties between the *wrong* side of the curtain and the *right* side of the top border. Topstitch all around the top border, ⅜in (1cm) from the edges.

Whipped running stitch, using two contrasting thread colours, produces a rope-like effect. Work the stitching about ⅛in (3mm) outside the heart.

Chain stitch provides a softer edging round some of the hearts.

For the French knots, match the thread colour to one of the colours used for the whipped running stitch edging.

For the running stitch, choose a cotton colour that matches or tones with the appliqué fabric.

Use radiating straight stitches to create bright starburst effects.

HEART TABLE MATS

These cheerful table mats, stencilled and stitched in vibrant colours to match the café curtain, create a bright setting for informal meals.

The finished mats are 19¾ x 11in (50 x 28cm) and have a 2¾in (7cm) wide heart panel at each side.

For each mat you need a 15½ x 12¼in (39 x 31cm) rectangle of the main fabric, and two blue 12¼ x 4in (31 x 10cm) rectangles. You also need Pebeo fabric paint in Vermilion, a stencil brush and masking tape, embroidery materials and equipment as listed on page 30, and matching sewing thread.

Preparing the stencil
The diagram (right) shows the heart stencil. You will need the smaller heart, shown in colour. Mask off any nearby cutouts.

Preparing the fabric
Fold each blue rectangle in half widthwise and finger press the fold. Open it out and finger press a crease 1¼in (3cm) from one long edge. Unfold the fabric and tape it on the prepared work surface with the short edges at the sides and the crease nearest to you.

Using a different colour for each heart, work chain stitch all round the outer edge.

Use a contrasting colour cotton to work a starburst of radiating straight stitches in the centre of each heart.

MAKING THE TABLE MATS

1 Centre the heart cutout on the creased centre line with the point on the horizontal crease. Stencil with Vermilion. Stencil a heart 1in (2.5cm) to the left and right of the first. Allow the paint to dry and fix it with a hot iron. ►

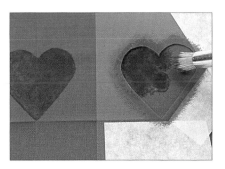

2 Using two strands of cotton (floss), work chain stitch around each heart, then work a star of radiating straight stitches in the centre (see left).

3 With the right sides together and taking ⅝in (1.5cm) seam allowances, stitch a heart panel to each end of the centre rectangle. Press the seam open. Press in ¼in (5mm), then ⅜in (1cm) all around and machine stitch.

MUSHROOMS

VELVETY MUSHROOMS IN PALE
COUNTRY HUES ARE STENCILLED
AND STITCHED ON KITCHEN
ESSENTIALS.

———————— ● ————————

YOU WILL NEED

- ❋ Mushroom stencil and stencil brush
- ❋ Pebeo fabric paints in White and Opaque Chamois
- ❋ White saucer
- ❋ Kitchen paper and wallpaper lining paper
- ❋ Masking tape
- ❋ DMC stranded cottons/floss as listed in colour key
- ❋ Embroidery needle, size 8
- ❋ Plain apron
- ❋ 5¾yd (5m) of 1in (2.5cm) wide pale brown cotton twill tape (if replacing straps and edging; 13½in [34cm] just for pocket)
- ❋ ¼yd (20cm) of heavyweight cotton fabric in cream (for pocket)

COLOUR KEY

COLOURS	SKEINS
703 Spring green	1
839 Dark coffee	1
840 Mid coffee	1
841 Coffee	1
842 Beige coffee	1

PAINT COLOUR GUIDE

For the mushroom caps and stalks: use White paint.

For the gills: mix Opaque Chamois with a little White to make dark mushroom paint.

MUSHROOM APRON

Giant button mushrooms stencilled and highlighted with easy stitching create a country feel on a simple kitchen apron.

Embellish a plain apron with a simple mushroom design. Either buy an apron with a large pocket or make the pocket yourself. You could even carry on the soft mushroom theme by using pale brown tape to cover or replace the neck and waist straps and to bind the edges.

Preparing the stencil

The diagram (right) shows the complete mushroom stencil. You will be using the group of large mushrooms shown in colour. Before you start, mask off any nearby cutouts.

Preparing the pocket

From the cream fabric: cut a piece 12½ x 8in (32 x 20cm). Fold it in half widthwise and tack along the fold. Lay the fabric out flat on the prepared work surface with the tacked line vertical.

STENCILLING

1 Mask off the gills. Centre the mushroom cutout in the right-hand half of the pocket, 1¼in (3cm) from the tacked line. Secure it with masking tape. Stencil the mushroom caps and stalks with White paint. ▲

2 Without lifting the stencil, remask to reveal the gills and stencil with dark mushroom paint. ▲

3 Clean, dry and flip the stencil. Position it on the left half of the pocket, 1¼in (3cm) from the tacked line. Repeat steps **1** and **2**. Let the paint dry and fix it with a hot iron. ▲

STITCHING

Following the stitch details (below) and using two strands of cotton (floss), add stem stitch outlines and satin stitch the gills. Add shaded seeding to give form to the mushroom caps and create blades of grass with fly and straight stitches.

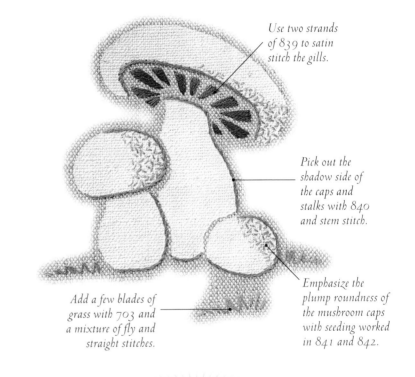

Use two strands of 839 to satin stitch the gills.

Pick out the shadow side of the caps and stalks with 840 and stem stitch.

Emphasize the plump roundness of the mushroom caps with seeding worked in 841 and 842.

Add a few blades of grass with 703 and a mixture of fly and straight stitches.

Attaching the pocket

After stencilling and stitching, sew pale brown tape to the top edge, like bias binding. Zigzag stitch the raw edges, fold them in ⅜in (1cm) and press. Centre on the apron, 9in (23cm) from the bottom, pin and topstitch around the edges and down the centre to divide the pocket in two.

RECIPE BOOK COVER

Give your best recipes a special home in a cookbook with a stencilled and stitched mushroom patch. On a 6in (15cm) square of linen, stencil the large mushroom group following steps **1-2** (above). Add stitching as for the apron pocket, then fray the edges of the fabric and glue it on to the book front.

MUSHROOM CLOTH

Line a basket with a linen mushroom cloth. The mushrooms have satin stitched gills, and bright green blades of grass add colour between the groups. The 17in (43cm) square cloth has a neatly bound edge.

You need a 19in (48cm) square of natural linen, fabric paint in White, a stencil brush, DMC stranded cottons (floss) in 703 and 839, dark tacking thread, needle, ⅜in (1cm) wide brown bias binding and matching sewing thread. You also need spray mount and a permanent black pen and ruler.

Preparing the stencil

You will be using the small mushrooms shown in colour (right).

Before you start, mask off any nearby cutouts and spray mount the back of the stencil, then leave it to dry. To help with positioning, use the ruler and permanent pen to draw a line along the bottom of the row of mushrooms, and short vertical lines at each end of the row.

Preparing the fabric

Tack a line all around the fabric 1¼in (4.5cm) in from each edge. Place the fabric flat on the work surface.

STENCILLING AND STITCHING

1 Start at the bottom left corner of the fabric. Align the drawn lines on the cutout with the tacked lines on the fabric. Stencil the mushrooms with White paint. Repeat to stencil the cutout ⅜in (1cm) to the right. ▼

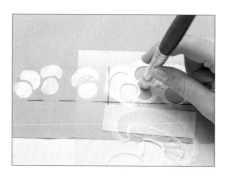

2 Turn the fabric through 90° and repeat step 1 (left) to stencil two sets of mushrooms on the next edge of the fabric square. Repeat twice more, then leave the paint to dry and fix it with a hot iron.

3 With two strands of cotton (floss), satin stitch the gills in 839, and work the grass in straight and fly stitch using 703. Trim ¾in (2cm) from the fabric all around, rounding the corners. Bind the edges with brown bias binding.

Leave the pairs of mushrooms as a paint effect.

Pick out the gills with satin stitch in 839.

Work blades of grass in straight and fly stitch using 703.

MOSAIC

DRAW INSPIRATION FROM THE ANCIENT
CIVILISATIONS OF THE MEDITERRANEAN
TO CREATE STENCILLED AND
STITCHED MOSAICS.

YOU WILL NEED

* Turquoise towel, large enough to cover the seat
* ¼yd (20cm) lime green cotton fabric
* Pebeo fabric paint in Transparent Light Green
* Stencil and stencil brush
* Kitchen paper and wallpaper lining paper
* Masking tape
* Spray mount
* DMC stranded cotton/floss as listed in the colour key
* Sewing thread to match the stranded cotton/floss
* Embroidery needle, size 7
* Hessian garden string
* Hessian fringing
* Bondaweb/WonderUnder
* Staple gun and staples or hammer and small nails
* Fabric glue (optional)

COLOUR KEY

COLOUR	SKEINS
3812 Turquoise	1

BATHROOM SEAT

A stencilled and stitched mosaic starfish seat cover gives an old bathroom seat a fresh new lease of life.

When you treat yourself to a new set of bathroom towels, buy an extra one to cover an old bathroom seat. Starfish are stencilled on to plain cotton fabric, embellished with simple stitching and then stitched on to the towel. Swirls of hessian string couched in place, and a matching hessian fringe, add to the fresh seaside feel.

The seat seen here is the old-fashioned type which doubles up as a laundry basket, but you can make the cover to fit any bathroom seat.

Preparing the stencil

The diagram (right) shows the mosaic stencil. For the seat cover you will need only the starfish cutout, shown here in colour, so mask off any cutouts close to it. Before you start, spray mount the back of the stencil and leave it to dry.

STENCILLING THE STARFISH

On the lime green fabric, use Transparent Light Green paint to stencil enough starfish to scatter over the required area for the stool cover. Space them at least 2in (5cm) apart. Allow the paint to dry and fix it with a hot iron. ➤

STITCHING THE COVER

1 Using three strands of 3812 and referring to the stitch details (right), work running stitch along the centre of each arm of the starfish, then add a French knot at the centre.

2 Centre the turquoise towel on the seat and use pins to mark the area needed to cover it, including the sides; allow about 2in (5cm) extra all around to turn under the seat. Using two strands of 3812, and referring to the stitch detail (top right), couch down random swirls of string all over the marked area.

3 Apply Bondaweb (WonderUnder) to the wrong side of the starfish fabric, and cut out each starfish ¼in (6mm) outside the stencilled design. Bond them on to the towel over the string. Machine zigzag stitch all around the starfish, using thread to match the stranded cotton (floss).

4 Stretch the towel over the seat and secure it underneath with small nails or staples. Stitch or glue the fringing in place.

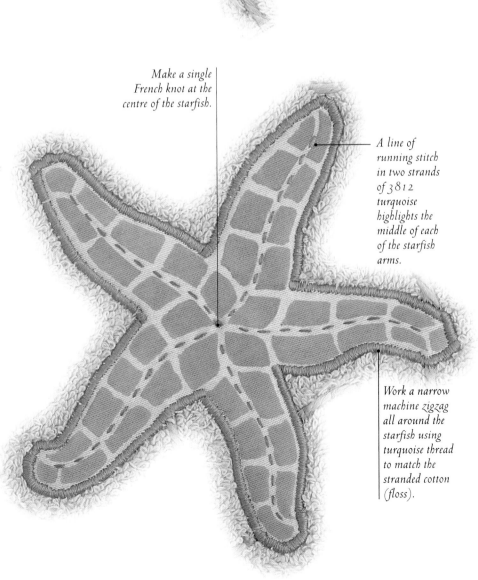

Couch down swirls of string, using the turquoise stranded cotton (floss).

Make a single French knot at the centre of the starfish.

A line of running stitch in two strands of 3812 turquoise highlights the middle of each of the starfish arms.

Work a narrow machine zigzag all around the starfish using turquoise thread to match the stranded cotton (floss).

YOU WILL NEED

* White waffle bath towel, at least 34 x 23in (86 x 58cm), with a 2¼in (6cm) deep woven border
* ⅞yd (80cm) of 36in (90cm) wide turquoise cotton fabric
* ¼yd (20cm) of white cotton fabric
* Pebeo fabric paint in White and Opaque Duck Blue
* Stencil and stencil brush
* White saucer
* Masking tape
* Kitchen paper and wallpaper lining paper
* Spray mount
* DMC stranded cottons/floss as listed in colour key
* Embroidery needle, size 7
* White and bright green sewing threads
* ¼yd (20cm) iron-on wadding/batting
* Large silver eyelets
* 1⅛yd (1m) cord

COLOURS	SKEINS
906 Apple	1
907 Pale apple	1
3808 Deep aqua	1
3812 Turquoise	1

PAINT COLOUR GUIDE

To make sea blue: mix Opaque Duck Blue with a little White.

To make light sea blue: mix sea blue (see above) with a little more White.

LAUNDRY BAG

A roomy drawstring bag made of gleaming white waffle fabric is the ideal hideaway for dirty laundry or bathroom clutter. The fabric is decorated with stencilled and lightly stitched mosaic waves and starfish – the stencilled and embroidered starfish are padded with iron-on wadding (batting), and then appliquéd on to the fabric for the bag. The circular-based bag is a softer, deeper version of the duffle bag featured on page 57. You can buy iron-on wadding (batting) in craft or department stores.

Preparing the stencil

You need all the cutouts from the mosaic stencil (below), so mask off as you work. Before you start, spray mount the back and leave it to dry.

Preparing the fabric

From the waffle towel: cut an 34 x 23in (86 x 58cm) rectangle with the woven towel border 1¼in (3cm) above the lower long edge. Tape the waffle fabric rectangle securely on to the prepared work surface with the woven border closest to you. The wave pattern is stencilled along the middle of the border.

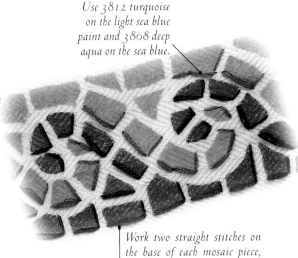

Use 3812 turquoise on the light sea blue paint and 3808 deep aqua on the sea blue.

Work two straight stitches on the base of each mosaic piece, and a single stitch on one side.

STENCILLING

1 Place one of the wave cutouts with the straight edge 6mm (¼in) from the lower edge of the towel border. Stencil it with sea blue paint. Move the stencil along and stencil again. Repeat along the length of the border. Allow the paint to dry. ▲

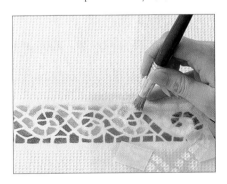

2 Position the other wave cutout so it fits into the first half of the design. Stencil it in light sea blue. Repeat along the length of the border as before. ▲

3 On the plain white cotton fabric, stencil one starfish with sea blue paint and two with light sea blue paint. Allow all the paint to dry and fix it with a hot iron.

STITCHING

1 Refer to the stitch details (above and below) and use two strands of cotton (floss) throughout. Work straight stitches to add shape to the edges of the wave mosaic border. Decorate the starfish with straight stitches and French knots.

2 Following the manufacturer's instructions, bond the iron-on wadding (batting) to the wrong side of the white cotton fabric. Cut out the starfish ¼in (6mm) outside the stencilled design and scatter them in the centre of the waffle fabric. Pin, then machine stitch in place with a small zigzag stitch using the bright green sewing thread.

3 Follow the instructions on page 57 to assemble the bag, but make it 21½in (55cm) deep and omit the wadding (batting), pockets, cord stays and the stitched casing. Line the bag with the turquoise fabric and fix the eyelets 2in (5cm) from the top edge.

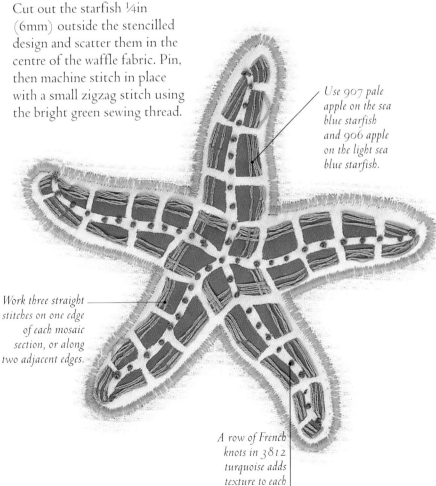

Use 907 pale apple on the sea blue starfish and 906 apple on the light sea blue starfish.

Work three straight stitches on one edge of each mosaic section, or along two adjacent edges.

A row of French knots in 3812 turquoise adds texture to each arm of the starfish.

TOWEL BANDS

Used on its own, the mosaic wave pattern makes a decorative design for towel bands to complete the nautical mosaic bathroom theme. Make the band as long as necessary to fit across your towels.

You will need cotton fabric to match your towel, the stencilling and embroidery materials and equipment listed on page 40, except stranded cottons (floss) 906 and 907. The towel design uses the two wave cutouts from the mosaic stencil, so mask off any nearby cutouts as you work.

Preparing the fabric

Cut a 4¾in (12cm) wide strip of plain cotton long enough to fit across the towel plus 2in (5cm). Finger press a lengthwise crease 1½in (4cm) from one long edge. Unfold the fabric and tape it on to the prepared work surface with the crease on the edge nearest to you.

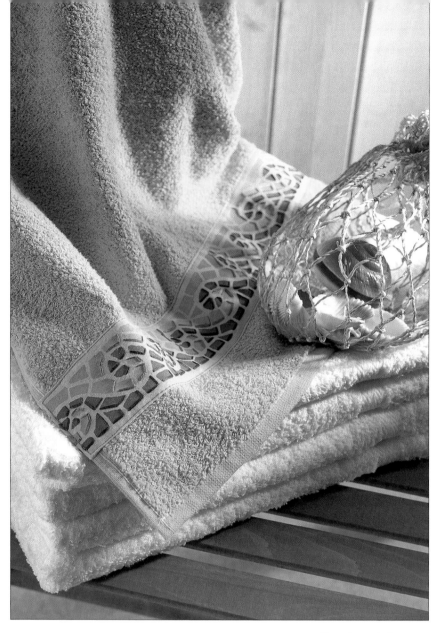

STENCILLING THE WAVE MOSAIC

1 Position one of the wave cutouts at one end of the fabric strip, with the straight edge on the crease. Stencil it in sea blue. Move the stencil along as often as required to stencil the length of fabric.

2 Fit the other wave cutout into the first half of the design and stencil it in light sea blue paint along the length of the fabric. Allow the paint to dry and fix it with a hot iron.

Straight stitch the waves as for the laundry bag on page 41.

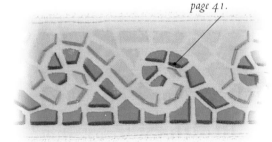

BRIGHT IDEAS

WAVE PURSE

Add a personal touch to a plain fabric make-up purse with a mosaic wave border. Stencil one half of the mosaic wave design in light sea blue paint, then embellish it with straight stitches as for the towel bands.

FINISHING THE BAND

Add straight stitch details to the mosaic, using two strands of cotton (floss) and referring to the details (above). Trim the long edges of the fabric ¾in (2cm) outside the design, and trim ⅜in (1cm) off each short end. Turn in ⅝in (1.5cm) all around and press. Pin, then topstitch the band in place on the towel using sewing thread to match the 3812 turquoise stranded cotton.

GOLDFISH

GLITTERING GOLDFISH GIVE
WATERY GLAMOUR TO
BATHROOM
ACCESSORIES.

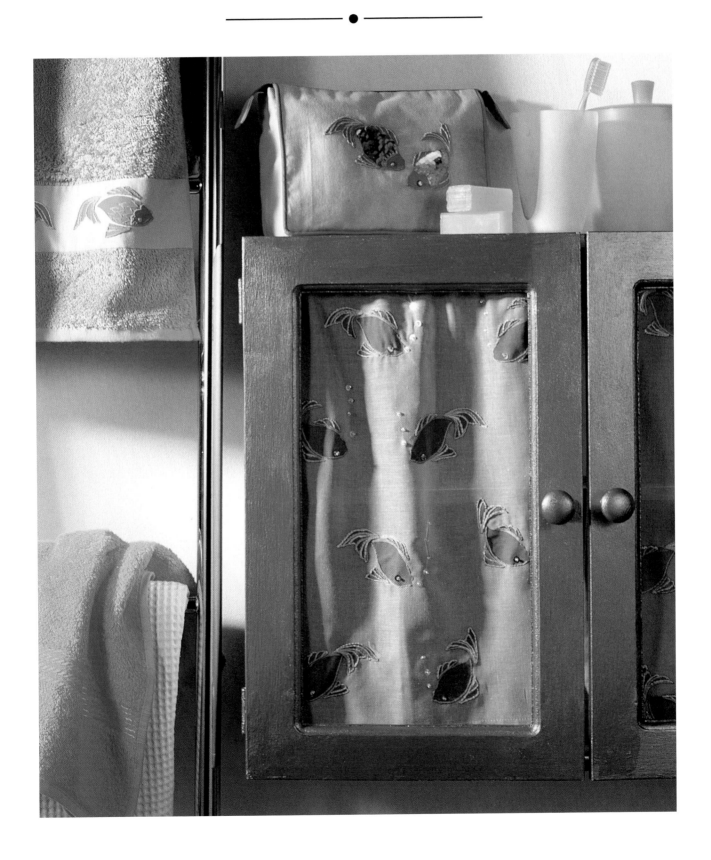

You Will Need

- ❋ ⅝yd (50cm) of 44in (112cm) wide cotton fabric in turquoise
- ❋ Pebeo fabric paints in Transparent Bright Orange and White
- ❋ Fish stencil and stencil brush
- ❋ White saucer
- ❋ Masking tape
- ❋ Spray mount
- ❋ Kitchen paper and wallpaper lining paper
- ❋ DMC stranded cottons/floss and rayon floss as listed in the colour key
- ❋ Orange sequins
- ❋ Clear glass beads
- ❋ Embroidery needle, size 7
- ❋ Embroidery hoop
- ❋ 11in (28cm) zipper
- ❋ Sewing thread to match the fabric
- ❋ 1½yd (1.4m) of thin piping cord
- ❋ 1½yd (1.4m) of orange bias binding

Colour Key

COLOURS	SKEINS
Stranded cotton/floss	
721 Rusty orange	1
Rayon floss	
30741 Tangerine	1
30742 Pale tangerine	1

Paint Colour Guide

To make mid orange: mix Transparent Bright Orange with a little White.

Goldfish Sponge Bag

A pair of goldfish with gleaming sequin scales decorates the front of a useful zipped bag.

The fins, tails and heads of the stencilled fish are picked out with glossy rayon floss threads, and their bodies are encrusted with dense overlapping rows of orange sequins to imitate their gleaming scales.

The sponge bag is trimmed with orange piping for a stylish finishing touch, and measures about 8¾ x 6¼in (22 x 16cm) with a 1½in (4cm) deep gusset. Full details on making the bag are given on pages 60–61.

Preparing the stencil
The diagram (right) shows the complete goldfish stencil. You will be using the two fish shown in colour, so mask off any nearby cutouts before you start. Spray mount the back of the stencil and allow it to dry.

Cutting out
Use the turquoise fabric for the outer bag and the lining.
For the side panels: cut four 10 x 7½in (25 x 19cm) pieces.
For the gusset: cut two 21¼ x 2¾in (54 x 7cm) pieces.
For the zipper tags: cut two 3¼ x 2in (8 x 5cm) pieces.

STENCILLING

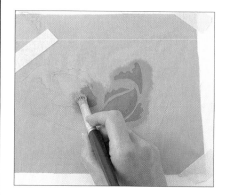

Tape a side panel on the work surface with the short edges at the sides. Centre the fish cutouts on the fabric with the tails nearest the top. Stencil them with mid orange. Allow the paint to dry and fix it with a hot iron. ▲

EMBROIDERING THE GOLDFISH

Using the stitch details (right) as a guide, work the stem stitch details on the fins and tails. Stitch the sequins in place then add the eyes, the body shadow and the mouth lines.

Finishing off
Make up the bag as described on pages 60–61, adding orange piping.

Use a single strand of rusty orange stranded cotton (floss) to attach the sequins. Start at the tail end and arrange them in overlapping rows to resemble scales.

Suggest the segments on the fins and tail with flowing stem stitched lines worked in two strands of rayon floss. Alternate tangerine and pale tangerine.

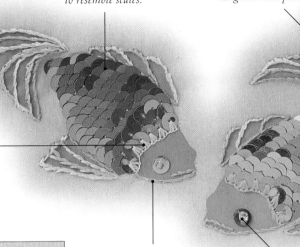

Attach the last row of sequins with a single strand of one of the rayon floss colours. Secure each sequin with three blanket stitches, so that the uprights radiate out from the centre hole.

Outline the mouth and the underside of the head with stem stitch and two strands of tangerine rayon floss.

For each eye, use the tangerine rayon floss to stitch on an orange sequin, securing it with a clear glass bead.

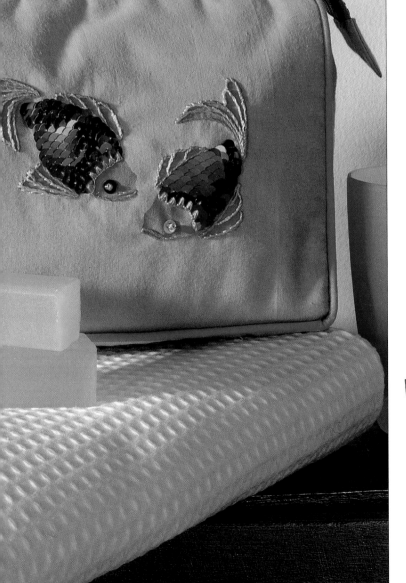

BRIGHT IDEAS

FISHY BAND

Brighten up a bathroom towel with a stitched and stencilled goldfish band. Cut a 3¾in (9.5cm) deep strip of turquoise fabric to fit across the towel plus 1¼in (3cm), and stencil pairs of fish along it using the mid orange paint. Stem stitch the details on the fins and tails, face and the edge of the head, then add fly stitches for the scales and French knots to suggest spots. Turn in ⅝in (1.5cm) all around the band and slipstitch the band on to the towel.

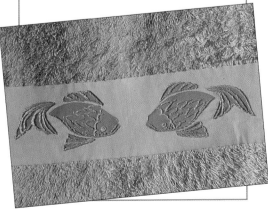

AQUARIUM CUPBOARD

A school of shimmering goldfish transforms a small cupboard into a bathroom aquarium. The fish are stencilled on to turquoise muslin and their fins and tails are picked out with shiny rayon floss threads. Their golden eyes and the trails of iridescent bubbles are picked out with beads and sequins.

You will need turquoise muslin, and the stencilling and stitching equipment listed on page 44. You will also need iridescent and orange sequins, clear glass beads and a reel of invisible nylon thread.

Preparing the stencil

The diagram (right) shows the complete goldfish stencil. You will need all the cutouts, so mask off any nearby cutouts before you start.

Preparing the fabric

Measure up for the curtains with the wires in place. Add 2¾in (7cm) to the finished length to find **A**. For the width multiply the length of the wire by 1½ to find **B**.
From the turquoise muslin: cut two curtains, each measuring **A** by **B**.

STENCILLING

Using all the fish cutouts, stencil the fish randomly over both curtains with mid orange. Allow the paint to dry and fix it with a hot iron. ▲

STITCHING

Refer to the stitch details (below) to stitch the fin and tail details and attach orange sequin eyes and iridescent bubbles.

Stitch ⅜in (1cm) double hems on the side edges of the curtains. At the top and bottom, turn in ⅜in (1cm) then 1in (2.5cm) and stitch to make casings. Thread the curtains on to the wires.

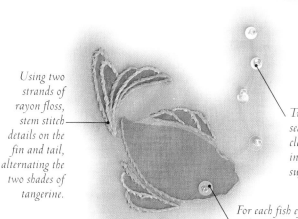

Stem stitch a shadow line on the body using two strands of rusty orange stranded cotton (floss).

Using two strands of rayon floss, stem stitch details on the fin and tail, alternating the two shades of tangerine.

Trails of iridescent sequins, secured with clear glass beads using invisible nylon thread, suggest the rising bubbles.

For each fish eye, use invisible nylon thread to stitch on an orange sequin, secured with a clear glass bead.

RIBBONS AND BOWS

RIBBONS AND BOWS IN SOFT SHADES OF BLUE BRING
A TOUCH OF ROMANCE TO THE BEDROOM.
USE SINGLE MOTIFS OR LINK THEM TO
CREATE A GRACEFUL GARLAND.

BEDLINEN GARLAND

Link bow motifs with flowing ribbons to create a border for the leading edge of a sheet. Embroider all or part of the border in satin stitch.

The garland of bows and ribbons is a delicate design, so choose a colour that stands out well against the white of the sheet. The darker areas of the bow shown here are satin stitched in two strands of deep blue; the paler areas use one strand each of light and mid blue. If you choose different colours, check your fabric paints on a scrap of white fabric first, and use this as a colour guide when you are choosing stranded cottons (floss) for the embroidery. The garland can be used to decorate a sheet of any size – just keep stencilling the design until you reach the edges.

Use either a cotton/polyester or a pure cotton sheet because these fabrics take stencil paint well. Wash and iron the sheet first, to remove creases and any manufacturer's finishes.

Mixing the paints

To make the blue shades to match the embroidery cottons (floss) listed, add a touch of Violet (see the paint colour guide left). The paints will darken a little as they dry. To keep the colours true, and the stencil brush clean, mix the paints with the tip of the brush handle or an old teaspoon. Wash your brush carefully and dry it when you change colour.

Preparing the stencil

The diagram (left) shows the ribbon and bows stencil. For the garland, you need the cutouts shown in colour – the small bow and the ribbon section, with its dots. Cover the other cutouts with masking tape.

Positioning the design

Along the lower short edge of the sheet, press a 3¼in (8cm) hem to the wrong side. To mark the centre, fold the sheet in half lengthwise and press the crease. Open out both the folds. *Note:* the garland may seem upside down when you stencil it. However, when the sheet is turned back, it will fall with the tails of the bows pointing towards the end of the bed. ▼

STENCILLING THE SHEET

1 Place the bow over the vertical centre crease, with the tail tips on the horizontal crease. Mark the position of the horizontal crease on the stencil. Use this mark to align the other bows. Stencil the bow with mid blue paint. Remove the stencil and wipe off any excess paint. ►

2 To position the ribbons, place the straight lower edge of the stencil on the horizontal crease. Stencil the dots and the first ribbon piece in mid blue. Repeat the procedure to stencil as many bows, ribbons and dots as you need to fit across the sheet.

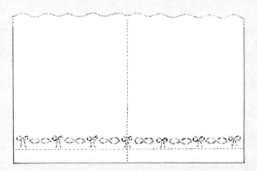

3 Remove tape and clean the stencil and brush. Tape the ribbon piece already stencilled, but don't tape the dots. Use the dots and edge of stencil to position the design. Use pale blue to stencil the dots again and the second ribbon piece. Leave to dry, then fix with an iron. ▲

STITCHING THE SHEET

To embroider the bows, use two strands of DMC 798 and satin stitch the main curve of the bow, as shown below. Use one strand each of 3753 and 809 to satin stitch the other curves of the bow and work the small sections of the garland. To hide the back of the embroidery, turn under a single 2¼in (6.5cm) hem and press. Slipstitch or machine stitch the hem in place.

To add depth to the design, use the darkest shade of blue as shown. Stitch all the bows in the garland using the same shading throughout to create a uniform effect.

Using one strand of 3753 and 809 together gives a subtle effect for the pale areas of stitching. The tails of the bow are left as a paint effect.

Use one strand each of blue 3753 and 809 to satin stitch the diamond shapes between the sections of ribbon.

The ribbon twists are stencilled in two shades of blue. Use small strips of tape to cover the section of ribbons you are not stencilling each time.

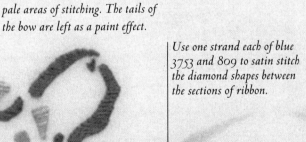

PILLOWCASE DESIGN

Decorate the corners of a pillowcase with the large bow and delicate trails of ribbon to match the sheet. A piece of card is inserted into the pillowcase to prevent the paint seeping through to the back of the pillowcase, and to give a firm stencilling surface. Set the motifs well in from the corners so that they sit forward when the pillow is inserted.

When stitching, try to keep a smooth edge along the outline.

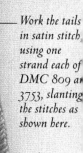

Satin stitch the pale blue areas using one strand each of DMC 809 and 3753.

Use two strands of deep blue DMC 798 to satin stitch the darker areas of the motif, making the stitches in the direction shown.

YOU WILL NEED

* White pillowcase, washed and ironed
* Stencil materials and one skein each of stranded cottons/ floss listed on page 48
* Large piece of card

Preparing the stencil

The diagram (right) shows the complete stencil. For the pillowcase, you need only the cutouts shown in colour. You use only the large bow and ribbon trails, so before you start, mask off the other cutouts.

Working the design

1 Slip the card inside the pillowcase and push it into the corner to be stencilled. With the centre of the large bow about 5in (12.5cm) in from the corner, stencil the motif with mid blue paint.

2 Position a trail of ribbon to one side of the bow and stencil it in light blue; repeat on the other side. Repeat the procedure to stencil the design in each corner. When the paint is dry, fix it with a hot iron.

3 Satin stitch the bow and tails as shown using two strands of cotton (floss).

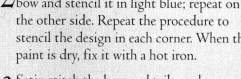

Work the tails in satin stitch using one strand each of DMC 809 and 3753, slanting the stitches as shown here.

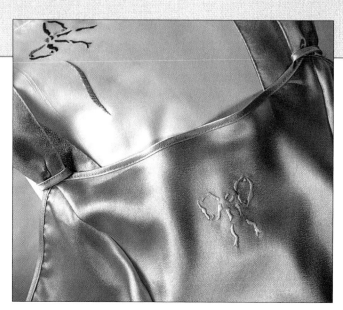

BRIGHT IDEAS

BOW BEAUTIES
If you want to satin stitch a complete motif there is no need to stencil it first – just draw inside the cutout with a sharp, hard pencil to create a stitching outline. The bow motif is shown here on a nightie, but it would look equally pretty on a blouse. On clothing, make sure the area to be stitched is easy to reach and free of bulky seams.

DAISIES

BRIGHT WHITE DAISIES SPARKLE LIKE JEWELS ON
SUMMER LAWNS. CAPTURE THEIR MIDSUMMER
GLORIES IN STITCHED AND STENCILLED ACCESSORIES
FOR YOUR BEDROOM.

YOU WILL NEED

* ⅝yd (50cm) of 36in (90cm) wide pale blue cotton fabric
* Daisy chain stencil and two stencil brushes
* Pebeo fabric paints in White, Opaque Light Green and Opaque Lemon Yellow
* White saucer
* Kitchen paper and wallpaper lining paper
* Masking tape
* Spray mount
* Anchor Marlitt threads as listed in the colour key
* Embroidery needle, size 8
* Embroidery hoop
* 2yd (1.8m) of thin white piping cord
* 2yd (1.8m) of white satin bias binding
* Zipper foot
* Cushion pad/insert, 15in (38cm) square

COLOUR KEY

COLOURS	SKEINS
800 White	1
810 Grass green	1
822 Gold	1
867 Yellow	1
1019 Pink	1
1029 Lime green	1
1030 Olive green	1

PAINT COLOUR GUIDE

For the stalks: mix Opaque Light Green with a touch of White and Opaque Lemon Yellow to make bright green.

For the flowers: use White.

DAISY CHAIN CUSHION

The perfect blue of clear summer skies provides the setting for pink-tipped daisies on a bedroom cushion.

Sweet daisy chains, stencilled on the cushion front, create a pretty border. The flowers are brought to life with gleaming Marlitt threads and simple stitching. For a fresh finish, the cover is trimmed with narrow white satin piping. It fits a 38cm (15in) square pad.

Preparing the stencil

The diagram shows the complete daisy stencil. You will be using the individual stem and flower cutouts, so mask off any others nearby. Before you start, spray mount the back of the stencil and allow it to dry.

Preparing the fabric

Cut a 16in (41cm) square of blue fabric. Press a crease 3⅛in (8cm) from each edge to give a 9¾in (25cm) square. Lay the fabric flat on the prepared work surface.

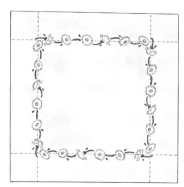

STENCILLING

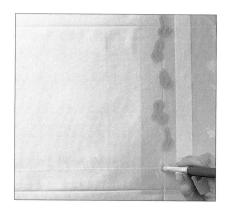

I Align the daisy stem cutouts along one edge of the creased square. Adjust the stencil so that the stems curve equally either side of the crease, and the end of the first stem projects beyond the square by ⅜in (1cm). Stencil the stems with bright green paint. Lift the stencil. ▲

EMBROIDERING THE DAISY CHAINS

Mount the stencilled fabric in the hoop and use a single strand of Marlitt thread throughout. Referring to the details (right), work the petals in long and short stitch and fill the flower centres with French knots. Satin stitch the stems.

Making the cushion cover

Measure round the piping cord and add 1¼in (3cm). Cut a strip of bias binding to this width, wrap it around the cord matching raw edges and machine stitch close to the cord using a zipper foot. Stitch it on to the cushion cover front and make up the cushion cover with an overlapped back, using the remaining blue fabric for the back. For details see page 59.

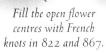

Fill the stems and leaves with slanted satin stitch using 810.

After filling the stem and calyx with 810, add satin stitches in 1030, at the very tip of the calyx.

Over the satin stitching, add single straight stitches in 1029. Arrange them so that they radiate out from the centre.

Pick out the pink petal tips with 1019. Change to white to finish the petals with stitches reaching to the base of the petal.

Fill the open flower centres with French knots in 822 and 867.

2 Position the daisy flower cutouts over the stencilled stems and stencil with White paint. ▲

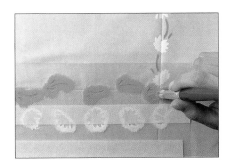

3 Repeat steps **1** and **2** to stencil the other three sides of the creased square. Allow the paint to dry and fix it with a hot iron. ▲

⌐ BRIGHT IDEAS ¬

DAISY PILLOWCASE

Complete the summer-fresh look with daisies scattered on sky blue bedlinen. Stencil individual daisies around the outer edge of a pillowcase, using bright green and White fabric paint as for the cushion cover. Using one strand of Anchor Marlitt thread, straight stitch the pink petal tips with 1019, and pick out the golden flower centres with French knots in 822 and 867. Define the inner curves of the stems with stem stitch worked in 810.

DAISY CHAIN DRAPE

A floaty curtain adds a delicate and breezy touch at the window or over your bed. You can buy ready-made ones in white Georgina from fabric and home furnishing stores. The stencilling instructions below are for one curtain. For a matching pair, flip the cutout and stencil the opposite edge of the second curtain.

You need the equipment and paint on page 52, yellow seed beads and Anchor Marlitt threads 810, 867 and 1019.

Preparing the stencil
The curtain uses the complete daisy chain stencil. Before you start, spray mount the back of the stencil and leave it to dry.

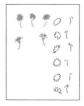

STENCILLING

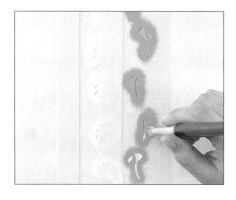

1 Position the daisy stem cutout at the top of the curtain, with the stems curving equally either side of the crease. Stencil the stems with bright green paint. ▲

2 Position the daisy flower cutout over the stems, and stencil them with White paint.

3 Working downwards, stencil more daisy chains in this way, spacing them carefully so that they appear to flow in a single chain. When dry, fix the paint with a hot iron.

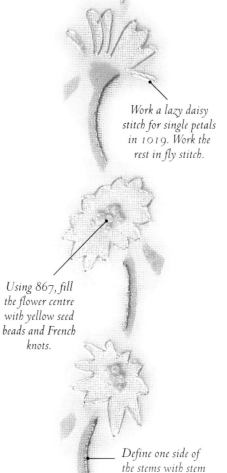

Work a lazy daisy stitch for single petals in 1019. Work the rest in fly stitch.

Using 867, fill the flower centre with yellow seed beads and French knots.

Define one side of the stems with stem stitch using 810.

EMBROIDERING THE DAISIES

Use a small embroidery hoop and follow the stitch details (left). Using one strand of Marlitt thread throughout, define the inner edge of each stalk with stem stitch, and outline the petals with fly and lazy daisy stitches. Use 867 to scatter French knots in the flower centres, and add yellow seed beads stitched on with the same thread.

CHAIR PROTECTORS

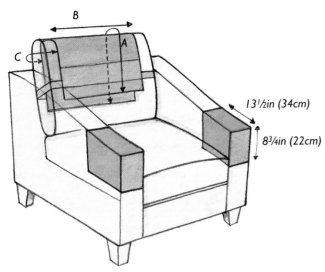

13½in (34cm)

8¾in (22cm)

Making the antimacassar

1 With right sides together, pin and stitch the contrast strip to the front edge of the main piece. Stitch the opposite edge of the contrast strip to the 4in (10cm) deep fabric strip. Press seams open.

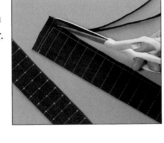

2 Fold the button straps in half lengthwise, with the right sides together. Stitch along one long and one short edge, trim the seam allowances turn right side out and press.

3 Place the main piece right side up. With raw edges together, pin a button strap to each side edge with the lower edge of the button strap level with the lower edge of the contrast strip. Tack in place.

4 Pin the main piece and the lining right sides together, and stitch all round, leaving a 3in (7.5cm) gap in the lower back edge. Trim the seam allowances, turn to right side and press. Slipstitch the gap closed.

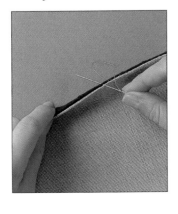

Measuring up

Antimacassar Decide on the length of the antimacassar (**A**) – remember that the back section is as long as the front. Decide on the width (**B**). To make the main pattern, cut a piece of paper **A** by **B**. Position the pattern over the back of the chair. Measure from the front edge of the pattern to the back side edge (**C**).

Armcap Use string to measure around the arm for the length of the main piece. For the front, cut a pattern 8¾in (22cm) deep by the width of the arm front.

Cutting out

Antimacassar From the contrast fabric, use the pattern to cut the lining, adding on ⅝in (1.5cm) all around. Cut one piece the same width by 6in (15cm) for the contrast strip. Cut two straps C plus 3¼in (8cm) by 5⅛in (13cm). From main fabric, cut the main piece the same width as the lining but 7½in (19cm) shorter; cut a second piece the same width by 4in (10cm).

Armcaps Cut two rectangles the string length plus 2¼in (6cm), by 15¼in (38.5cm). For the front, use the pattern to cut two pieces, adding ⅝in (1.5cm) on the side and top edges and 1¼in (3cm) at the lower edge.

Making the armcaps

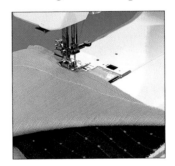

1 Right sides together, pin one long edge of the main piece around the side and top edges of the front piece, clipping the curves and corners. Stitch. Trim and neaten seam.

2 On all remaining raw edges, press under ⅜in (1cm) then ¾in (2cm), trimming the corners to reduce bulk. Pin and stitch close to the fold.

5 Work a buttonhole at the free ends of each button strap. Lapping the button strap over the back edge by 2in (5cm), sew a button to each side of the back to correspond with the buttonholes.

COVERING SEAT PADS

Most seat pads have a foam pad and wadding (batting), which may be protected by calico or hessian. Stretch the new cover over the top, and staple to the underside with a staple gun, or tacks and a hammer.

If the seat has lost its bounce, ask a foam supplier to cut you a new piece of foam. Glue it on to the base with a PVA adhesive and cover with mediumweight wadding (batting) before adding the fabric cover.

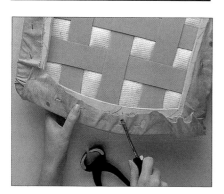

1 Remove the seat pad and place it wrong side up on the work surface. Prise out the staples or tacks with a screwdriver and pliers or use a staple remover. Take off the backing cloth. Remove the fabric cover in the same way.

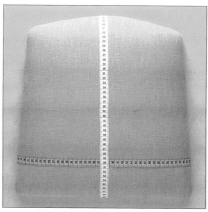

2 Measure the width of the seat from one base edge to the opposite base edge (**A**). Measure the depth from the front base edge to the back base edge (**B**). Cut a piece of fabric **A** plus 2in (5cm) by **B** plus 2in (5cm).

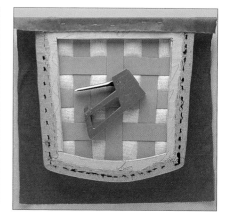

3 Centre the seat pad on the wrong side of the fabric. Staple the fabric to the centre back. Working out from the centre, add more staples, spacing them about ½in (4cm) apart. Stop 2in (5cm) from the corners.

4 Turn the pad round, and pull the fabric tightly to the front edge. Staple it in place from the centre out. Repeat to secure the sides.

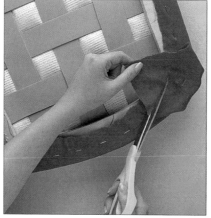

5 At each corner, pull the fabric tightly to the back and staple in place. Trim off the point with scissors.

7 Cut a piece of base cloth to fit the base. Lay it on the underside, turning under the edges so that they conceal the raw edges and staples on the top cover. Staple in place. ➤

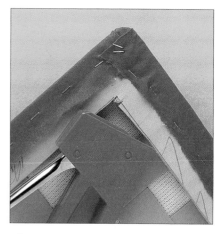

6 Fold the tucks of fabric over the corner and staple them down.

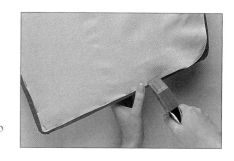

MAKING A PADDED DUFFLE BAG

1 Tack the wadding (batting) to the wrong side of the outer bag pieces and machine stitch.

2 On the top short edge of the pocket piece, press under ⅝in (1.5cm) then 1¼in (3cm) and stitch. Press under ⅝in (1.5cm) on the other edges. Centre the pocket on the right side of the outer fabric rectangle, 4in (10cm) above the lower edge. Stitch along the sides and bottom.

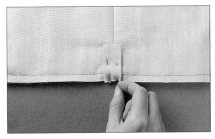

3 Join the short edges by folding in half widthwise, right sides together and pinning. Stitch ¾in (2cm) from the top edge and press the seam allowances open. Fold the tab piece in half lengthwise, right sides together and stitch the long edges. Turn right side out, fold in half, pin and tack it over the seam on the right side of the lower edge of the bag, as shown.

Cutting out

From fabric, lightweight wadding (batting) and lining: cut a 11½in (29cm) diameter circle for the base and a 33⅞ x 19in (86 x 48cm) rectangle for the sides. *From fabric only:* cut a 8¾ x 6¾in (22 x 17cm) rectangle for the pocket; a 4¼ x 3¼in (11 x 8cm) rectangle for the tab; and a 6¼ x 3¼in (16.5 x 8cm) rectangle for the cord stay.

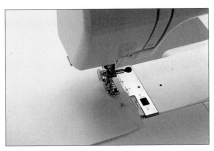

4 With the right sides together, pin and tack the base to the lower edge of the bag. Stitch, then remove the tacking. Clip the curves. Make a second bag from the lining fabric, leaving a 5in (12.5cm) gap in centre of seam to turn through. Turn lining the right way out and slip into the bag, so that the right sides are together. Pin then stitch the upper edges. Turn the bag right side out through the opening. Slipstitch closed and press the upper edge.

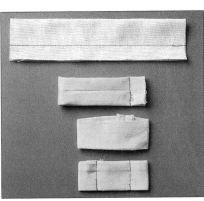

5 Fold the cord stay piece in half lengthwise, right sides together; stitch the long edges. Turn out, then stitch the short ends together. Trim the seam allowances and turn it to the inside. Fold the stay with the seam ⅝in (1.5cm) from one end. Stitch across ⅝in (1.5cm) from each end to make slots.

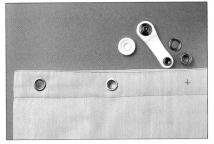

6 For the casing, stitch close to the upper edge of the bag, then 1½in (3.5cm) below. Use an air-erasable pen to mark the positions for an even number of eyelets 4⅛in (10.4cm) apart in the middle of the casing. Follow the manufacturer's instructions to insert the eyelets.

7 Cut 64in (163cm) of cord. Thread it through the tab, the stay and the eyelets as shown. Bind the ends together with sticky tape. Cut 1¾ x 1½in (4.5 x 4cm) of fabric and press under ⅜in (1cm) on the short edges. Wrap the fabric tightly round the sticky tape and stitch firmly in place.

TAB CURTAINS

Calculating fabric amounts

Fix the pole at least 3½in (8cm) above the window to allow for the tabs. Measure from 1¼in (3cm) below the pole to the required length of the curtain – this is the finished curtain length. Add on 4⅝in (11.5cm) to allow for the hem and the top turning – this is the cut length.

To work out the cut tab length, measure round the pole and add on 3¼in (8cm). To the cut length add 4in (10cm) for the facings, and for self tabs add the cut tab length – this is the total length.

For the curtain width, multiply the length of the pole by 1½ – for two curtains, divide the total by two to find the width of each curtain. To calculate how many fabric widths you need, divide the curtain width by the width of your fabric and round up the answer. To find the total amount of fabric required, multiply the total length by the number of fabric widths.

Cutting out

From furnishing fabric: cutting straight across the width of the fabric, cut lengths equal to the cut length. Cut the required number of widths. For the tabs, cut strips to the cut tab length by twice the finished tab width, plus ¾in (2cm). For the facing, cut 4in (10cm) deep strips across the fabric width. Cut one for each curtain width.

From interfacing: cut the same number of interfacing strips as facing strips, but make them ⅜in (1cm) smaller all around.

1 Join fabric widths to make up the curtains; press the seam allowances open. If there is more than one fabric width in the curtain, join facing strips to match. On the side edges of each curtain, press ⅜in (1cm), then ¾in (2cm) to the wrong side. Stitch close to inner fold.

2 Along the bottom edge, turn 1in (2.5cm), then 3in (7.5cm) to the wrong side and press. Fold the corners of the hem in at an angle until they align with the side hems. Stitch along the hem close to the fold, up to the side hem. Slipstitch neatly along the folded corners.▶

3 With the right sides together, fold each tab in half lengthwise. Stitch the long edge, taking a ⅜in (1cm) seam allowance. Centre the seam; press with seam allowances open. Turn tabs right side out and press again.

4 Lay out the main curtain fabric right side up. Pin a folded tab to each end of each top edge, with the raw edges matching. Fold the remaining tabs and pin and tack them evenly in between.▶

5 Neaten one long edge of the facing strips with machine zigzag stitch. Then fuse the interfacing centrally to the wrong side. Turn a 1in (2.5cm) hem to the wrong side along the neatened edge of the facing and stitch close to the inner edge.

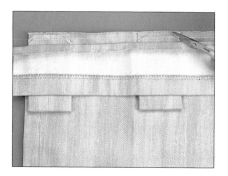

6 With the wrong side facing up and the raw edges matching, lay the facing over the tabs. Tack, then stitch across the curtain top, through the facing, the tabs and the main fabric, taking a ⅝in (1.5cm) seam allowance.

7 Trim the ends of the tabs, layering them and clipping diagonally across the corners to reduce bulk. ▲

8 Turn the facing to the wrong side of the curtain and press it. Press under the raw edges of the facing at each end of the curtain and slipstitch them to the curtain's side hem. ▲

EASY CUSHION COVERS

The easiest type of cushion cover to make is a square or rectangular shape with an overlapped back opening. Use fabrics that are closely woven, crease-resistant and durable. Strong furnishing fabrics made of cotton and linen blends are ideal. See the 'You Will Need' boxes for fabric recommendations.

Cut out the front and back pieces separately, and stencil and work the design before assembling the cushion.

To hold the pad firmly in place, the cover needs a generous overlap at the back. The steps below explain how to make a cover with a 4in (10cm) wide overlap, which suits cushions up to 13¾in (35cm) square. For larger ones, the overlap needs to be at least 6in (15cm), so

cut the back piece 8¼in (21cm) wider than the front.

On a rectangular cover, position the back overlap so that it runs widthwise (parallel to the two shorter sides) to ensure that it holds its shape.

When you have finished stitching the cover (step **4** below), turn it to the right side and insert the pad.

Attaching piping

If piping is to be attached, stitch it to the outer edges at stage **2** (below). Tack the piping to right side of the cover front, leaving ⅝in (1.5cm) free at the start and 2in (5cm) at the end to overlap. Machine stitch close to the tacking using a zipper

foot. To ease round corners, clip into the seam allowances. Stop stitching ⅜in (1cm) from the end. Leaving the needle in the fabric, cut off the end of the cord so it overlaps the start by 1in (2.5 cm). Unpick 1in (2.5cm) of stitching from the end of the piping. Trim the cord end so it meets the start. Fold under ⅜in (1cm) on the overlapping fabric end. Lap it over the other end and finish stitching the piping in place.

MAKING A CUSHION WITH AN OVERLAPPED OPENING

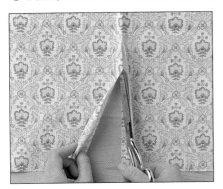

I Cut the fabric for the front piece ⅝in (1.5cm) larger all round than the finished cushion. Cut the fabric for the back piece 6¼in (16cm) wider than the front. Cut the back piece in half widthwise.

2 Turn, press and machine stitch a ⅝in (1.5cm) double hem along the centre edge of each back piece.

3 With right sides together, pin the back pieces to the front. Make sure that the raw edges match all round and the hemmed centre back edges overlap by about 4in (10cm).

4 Stitch around the outer edge, taking ⅝in (1.5cm) seam allowances. Stitch twice across each end of the overlap for strength. Trim the corners of seam allowances diagonally.

BOX BAGS

These stylish box bags look really professional, yet they are very simple to make. A fabric gusset stitched between the front and back panels provides depth and creates a neat, roomy box shape, ideal for storing bulky items such as toiletries.

The bags can be made in any size or shape, with or without piping. A large version makes a handy wash bag, while a tall, narrow shape is just right for make-up brushes. For a coordinated look, make a set of three to match your bathroom and fill them with toiletries, such as shampoo bottles, toothbrushes and tweezers – the perfect way to keep bathroom clutter out of the way.

For the best results, make your box bag from closely woven, washable fabrics. Use ready-made piping or make your own.

> **YOU WILL NEED**
> ❋ Main fabric
> ❋ Piping (optional)
> ❋ Piping foot (optional)
> ❋ Zipper foot
> ❋ Lining fabric
> ❋ Zipper
> ❋ Tacking thread and needle
> ❋ Matching thread

Cutting out

Decide on the height of the side panel (**A**) and the width (**B**), and how wide to make the gusset (**C**). *From main fabric and lining:* for the side panels cut two pieces **A** plus 1¼in (3cm) by **B** plus 1¼in (3cm). For the gusset cut one piece twice A plus **B** by **C** plus 1¼in (3cm). *From main fabric only:* cut two pieces 3¼ x 2in (8 x 5cm) for the zipper tags.

For a washbag or make-up bag, make the lining from a waterproof, wipe-clean fabric for easy care. Shower curtain material, available from fabric and department stores, is ideal.

1 Press ⅝in (1.5cm) to the wrong side along the top edges of the side panels: unfold. Tack the piping round the lower three edges so the tacking is ⅝in (1.5cm) in from the edges. Snip into the flat part of piping at the corners so that it lies flat.

2 Using either a zipper or piping foot on your sewing machine, stitch the piping in place with matching thread; start and finish the stitching at the foldline. At the corners, raise the presser foot, leaving the needle in the fabric and pivot the work.

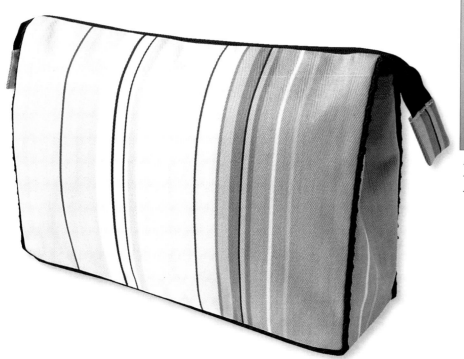

3 Press in ⅝in (1.5cm) on the short edges of the gusset; stitch. Place the gusset to a side panel with the top edges of the gusset 1¼in (3cm) below the top of the side panel. Snip at the lower corners to fit. Tack then stitch in place with a zipper or piping foot. Stitch the other edge of the gusset to the other panel in the same way.

4 Press in ⅜in (1cm) on the short edges of the zipper tags. Fold the tags in half, right sides together, and stitch the side edges ⅜in (1cm). Trim the seam allowances to ¼in (5mm).

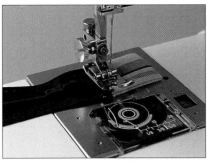

5 Turn the tags right side out. Tuck each end of the zip tape inside a tag, on top of the seam allowances. Machine stitch in place, finishing off the thread ends securely.

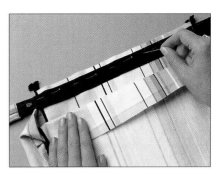

6 With the bag inside out, centre the zipper along one top edge, right sides together. Tack the zipper tape in place along the foldline. Stitch using the zipper foot.

7 Tack and stitch the other zipper tape to the other top edge in the same way. Remove the tacking.

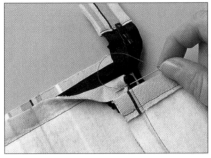

8 Turn the bag right side out. At the top corners of the side panels fold down the seam allowance and tuck the end of the piping underneath. Oversew by hand to secure.

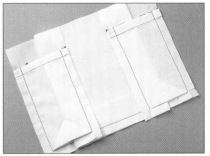

9 Trim ¾in (2cm) from one short end of the lining fabric gusset. Stitch the lining panels as in step 3 on page 60 but place the top of the gusset 1½in (4cm) down from the top edges of the side panels.

The standard zipper tag size suits most box bags, including miniature versions (below). On a tall, narrow version, like the make-up brush bag (left), longer tags suit the slimline look. For tags like these, cut two 4¾ x 2in (12 x 5cm) fabric pieces.

10 Place the lining inside the bag, with the wrong sides together. Pin the lining gussets ⅜in (1cm) below the main gussets. Tuck in the raw edge of the lining to fit, then pin and handstitch it in place.

STITCH LIBRARY

THIS CHAPTER CONTAINS ALL THE STITCHES USED IN THE PROJECTS, GROUPED TOGETHER FOR EASE OF REFERENCE.

SATIN STITCH

Starting and finishing off satin stitch

When you have finished satin stitching a motif, always secure the thread ends and trim them off before working the next motif. Don't trail the thread across the back of the work to start another motif – it may show through as a shadow on your finished work, especially on lightweight or pale fabric.

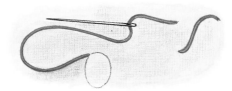

1 A little way from your starting point, push the needle through to the back of the fabric, leaving a 3in (7.5cm) tail of thread on the right side. Bring the needle out to the front again at your starting point on the edge of the motif.

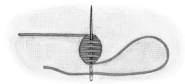

2 When you have filled in the motif, take the thread through to the back. Weave it into the back of your stitching, and trim it off close to the surface. Then pull the first thread end to the wrong side, weave it in and trim it off in the same way.

Filling a rounded shape with basic satin stitch

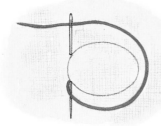

1 Bring the needle out at the front of the fabric at the edge of the shape. Insert the needle at the opposite edge, and bring it out again next to where you started.

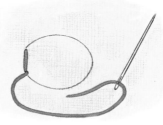

2 Pull the thread through gently, so that it runs straight between the marked lines without wavering; it should lie smoothly against the surface of the fabric, without puckering it.

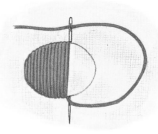

3 Repeat steps **1-2**, keeping the stitches parallel and close together so that they lie neatly and evenly on the surface of the fabric.

Working a basic satin stitch line

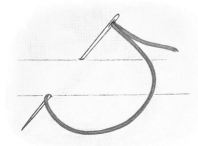

1 Bring the needle out at the front of the fabric at the lower marked line. Take the thread upwards and insert the needle on the top row, at a 45° angle to the marked line; bring it out again next to where you started.

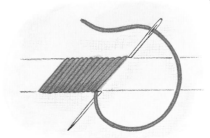

2 Work parallel, closely spaced stitches along the row, keeping them at exactly the same angle and placing the needle precisely on the marked lines to create even edges.

WHAT WENT WRONG

Loose stitches
Loose, untidy satin stitches are created when working the stitch over an area which is too large. For the best results, each stitch should be no more than ⅜-½in (10-12mm) long. For large areas use encroaching satin stitch, worked in manageable rows.

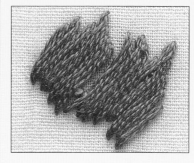

STRAIGHT STITCH

Securing your starting thread

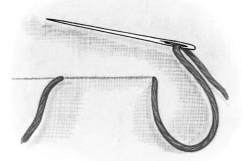

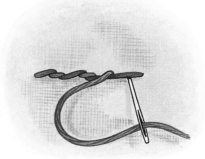

Finishing off

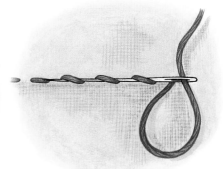

1 Push the needle to the back of the fabric, a little way from your starting point. Leave a short tail of thread at the front. Bring the needle to the front at your starting point.

2 As you work along the line, stitch over the thread at the back to secure it. Then pull the loose thread end through to the back and snip it off close to the surface.

To secure the thread end when you have finished, push the needle to the back of the fabric. Weave the thread into the back of several stitches and trim it off close to the surface.

Working basic straight stitch

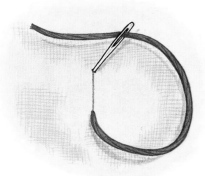

To work an individual straight stitch, bring the needle out to the front. Push it through to the wrong side to make a single stitch of the required length.

To work a cluster of straight stitches, work individual straight stitches of varying lengths and in different directions according to the design.

To create a simple straight stitch flower, make as many straight stitches as desired, working outwards from a central circle or oval.

STAR FILLING STITCH

Working star filling stitch

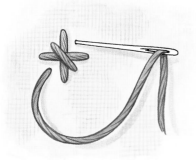

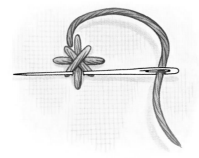

1 Work a large St George cross stitch, as shown above. Then work an ordinary cross stitch over the top. Make both crosses the same size.

2 Work a tiny ordinary cross stitch over the top of the large crosses to anchor them.

WHAT WENT WRONG

Tension too tight Untidy areas of open filling stitches are caused when the thread is pulled too tightly. For a neat finish, try to make all the stitches the same size and keep the tension of the thread constant as you move from stitch to stitch.

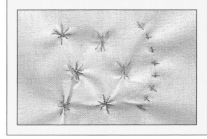

STRAIGHT STITCH

Working running stitch

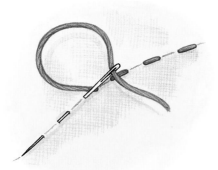

Working from right to left, bring the needle out to the front at your starting point. Pass the needle in and out of the fabric along the stitching line. Work several stitches at a time, keeping the length and tension even.

Working whipped running stitch

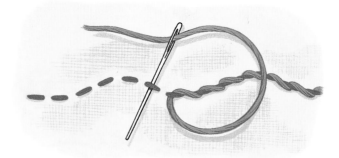

I Work a foundation row of running stitch with the stitches closer together than usual.

2 Using a tapestry needle, bring the whipping thread to the front at the beginning of the foundation row. Whip the thread over and under the running stitches without going through the fabric.

Working stem stitch

I Work upwards, keeping the working thread to the right. Bring the needle out to the front and insert it a little way from your starting point. Bring it out again, half a stitch length back.

2 Insert the needle half a stitch length from the end of the previous stitch. Bring it out at the end of the previous stitch, through the same hole in the fabric. Continue in this way.

For a heavy stem stitch line, angle the needle slightly as you insert it, and work smaller stitches.

Working backstitch

I Working from right to left, bring the needle out to the front one stitch length from your starting point. Insert the needle at your starting point and bring it out again, two stitch lengths away.

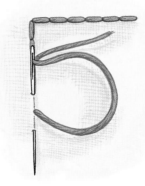

2 Pull the thread through to leave a single stitch at the front. Then repeat step 1, inserting the needle in the hole at the end of the previous stitch. Continue in this way, keeping all the stitches the same length.

WHAT WENT WRONG?

Ragged stems
Stem stitch looks ragged and untidy when the stitches are too long and the needle is not inserted along the centre of the line to make each stitch. Keep the stitches small and make them all the same length to ensure a smoothly stitched line.

LAZY DAISY STITCH
Working lazy daisy stitch

1 Bring the needle through to the front of the fabric. Insert the needle beside the emerging thread and bring it out to the front again a stitch length away, looping the working thread under the point of the needle.

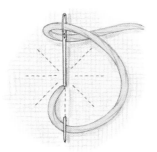

2 Pull the thread so that the loop lies flat. Make a short straight stitch over the loop to anchor it. Bring the needle out to the front ready to begin the next stitch.

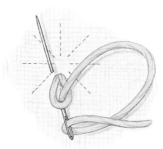

FLY STITCH
Working fly stitch

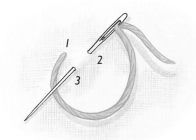

1 Bring the needle to the front at 1. Insert it to the right at 2. Angle the needle and bring it out over the working thread at 3.

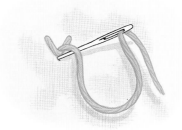

2 Pull the needle through and make a vertical stitch over the loop to anchor it to the fabric.

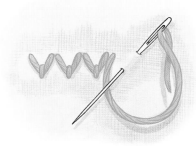

3 To make a horizontal row of fly stitches, bring the needle to the front at the top right of the first stitch and repeat steps **1-2** along the row.

CROSS STITCH
Working individual counted cross stitch

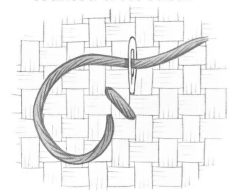

Bring the needle out at the front of the fabric and insert it one hole down and one hole to the right. Pull the thread through. Bring the needle out one hole to the left and insert it one hole up and one to the right.

SEED STITCH
Working seed stitch

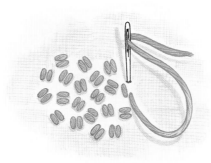

Work tiny straight stitches in pairs, scattering them over the fabric at different angles.

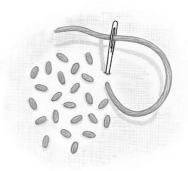

Alternatively, scatter single straight stitches randomly for a lighter look.

LONG AND SHORT STITCH

Working long and short stitch

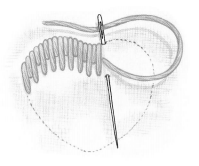
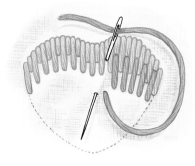
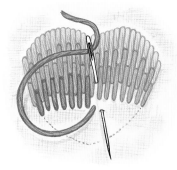

1 Work the foundation row in alternate long and short stitches, working from left to right and following the outline of the shape to be filled. Work the stitches close together.

2 Work the second row from right to left, filling in the spaces left by the first row and keeping the stitches all the same length.

3 Work subsequent rows alternately from left to right and right to left, keeping all the stitches the same length, as in step **2**. Change thread colour as you work for a subtle blended effect and work stitches closely so no background fabric shows.

HERRINGBONE STITCH

Starting and finishing herringbone stitch

1 To start, leave a 2-4in (5-10cm) tail of thread at the front to the left of your starting point. Work two or three running stitches, then bring the thread to the front at your starting point.

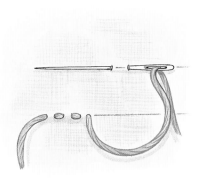

2 To finish, take the needle to the back and darn in the thread end under several stitches. Return to the beginning of the row and unpick the running stitches. Darn in the thread end at the back.

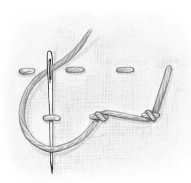

Working basic herringbone stitch

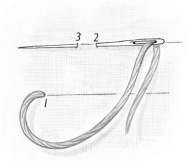
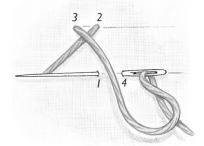
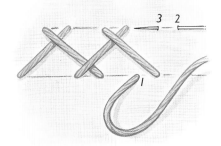

1 Bring the thread to the front of the fabric at the left-hand edge of the lower line at 1. Make a slanting stitch to the top right, inserting the needle at 2. Bring the needle to the front again a short distance to the left at 3.

2 To complete the first cross, make a slanting stitch towards the lower line, inserting the needle at 4. Bring the needle to the front at 1, directly below 2, ready to work the second cross.

3 Repeat the 1, 2, 3, 4 sequence along the row, making sure you keep the spacing and the length of the individual crosses perfectly even all the way along the row.

BLANKET STITCH

Securing the thread

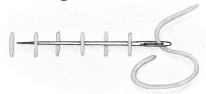

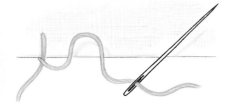

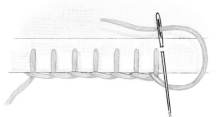

Method A Push the needle through to the front at your starting point, leaving a short tail of thread at the back. Work a few stitches, then turn the fabric over and weave the loose thread into the back of the stitches. To finish, fasten off the thread in the same way.

1 Method B Use this method for edging appliqué and fabric edges. To start, insert the needle at the top edge of the stitching line, leaving a tail of thread at the front. Take the working thread over the loose thread, ready to work the next stitch.

2 Work the row of stitches, then take the thread to the back. Make two or three tiny stitches on top of each other, next to the last upright and taking the needle through the background fabric only. Finish off the thread at the start in the same way.

Working blanket stitch for surface embroidery

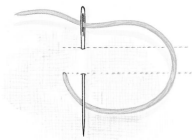

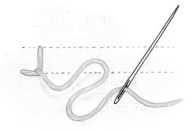

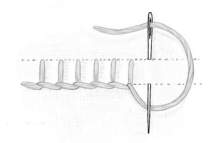

1 Bring the needle to the front on the lower line and insert it at the top, a little way to the right. Bring it out directly below, keeping the thread under the tip of the needle .

2 Pull the thread through the fabric, over the top of the working thread. Gently pull the thread to form a firm loop at the lower line.

3 Continue working in this way, spacing the upright stitches evenly and making them all the same height.

Working blanket stitch round a curved shape

1 Work blanket stitches round the shape, with the loops on the outside and the uprights facing towards the centre.

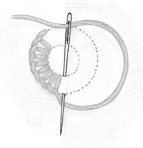

2 When you have stitched all round, work the last upright. Take the needle back through the fabric at the point where it originally emerged.

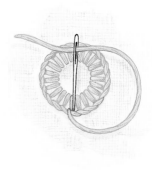

FEATHER STITCH

Working feather stitch

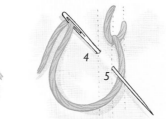

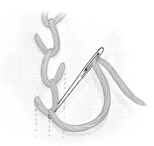

1 Mark three parallel vertical lines on your fabric. Bring the needle to the front at 1 and insert it at 2. Angle the needle and bring it to the front at 3 over the working thread. Pull the needle through to complete the first stitch.

2 Insert the needle lower down on the left-hand line at 4, angle the needle and bring it out to the front on the centre line at 5 over the working thread. Pull the needle through to complete the second stitch.

3 Repeat steps 1-2, alternating the looped stitches to the left and to the right of the centre line. At the end of the row, make a small vertical stitch over the last loop and secure the thread.

FRENCH KNOT
Working a French knot

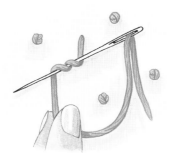

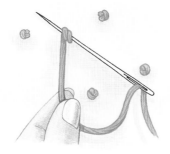

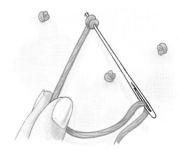

1 Bring the thread through to the front of the fabric. Holding the thread taut with your left hand, wrap it twice round the needle.

2 Pull the thread gently to tighten the twists round the needle. Don't overtighten the twists, or you will find it difficult to slide the needle through in the next step.

3 Keeping the thread taut, insert the needle into the fabric close to the point where it originally emerged. Pull the needle and thread through to the back, to leave a loose knot at the front.

Starting and finishing knotted stitches

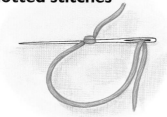

To start, work two or three tiny stitches at the back of the fabric, positioning them where they will be covered by the embroidery stitch. To finish, fasten off the thread in the same way, directly beneath the knot. Trim the thread close to the fabric. When you are working individual knots or widely spaced knots, fasten off the thread after each knot. When working groups of closely spaced knots, you can carry the thread across the back of the fabric between knots, instead of fastening it off after every stitch.

BULLION KNOT
Working a bullion knot

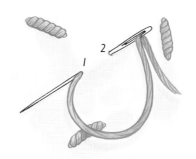

1 Bring the needle through to the front (1). Insert the point of the needle a short way back (2), and bring the needle to the front again where it originally emerged (1). Don't pull the thread through.

2 Holding the working thread taut with your left hand, wrap it round the needle point five to seven times to make a coil of twists.

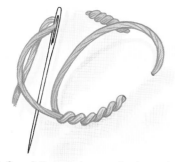

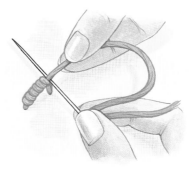

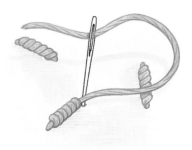

3 Carefully pull the needle through both the fabric and the twists on the needle, taking care not to distort the twists. This stage may take some practice to perfect.

4 Gently pull the thread back so that the coil of twists lies flat on the fabric. Then tighten the thread and use the point of the needle to pack the twists together evenly.

5 To finish the knot, take the needle and thread back through the fabric at position 2.

COUCHING

Starting off couching

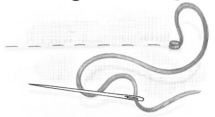

1 Start at the right hand end of the couching line. Secure the couching thread first with a few backstitches. Place them where they will be covered by the laid thread. Leave a 2in (5cm) tail of thread at the back of the fabric.

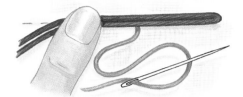

2 Place the laid thread on the fabric, leaving an extra 2in (5cm) at the start of the couching line. Hold the laid thread in place with your left thumb.

Finishing off couching

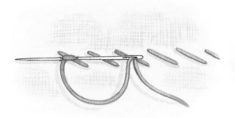

To finish off the couching thread, take it to the back of the fabric. Secure it with a few stitches beneath the laid thread. Leave a 2in (5cm) tail of couching thread. Then cut off the laid thread, leaving a 2in (5cm) tail.

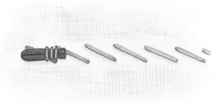

To secure a fine or mediumweight laid thread, thread the end on to a large-eyed needle and gently take it through to the back of the fabric. At the back, fold the end over the row of stitching. Then secure it with a few stitches, using the couching thread.

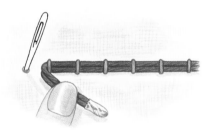

To secure a thick laid thread, make a small hole in the fabric with a large needle or the point of a stiletto. Wrap sticky tape round the end of the laid thread and poke it carefully through the hole and pull it to the back. Secure as for a fine or mediumweight thread.

Working basic couching

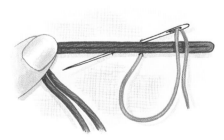

1 If you are using two strands of laid thread, fold a single length in half and position it on the fabric with the strands side by side. Bring the couching thread to the front, just below the laid thread. Make a tiny vertical stitch over the laid thread. Bring the needle to the front again a short distance to the left.

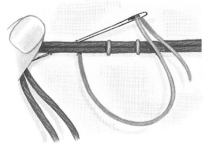

2 Continue making vertical stitches over the laid thread until it is anchored to the fabric along its length. Space the stitches evenly.

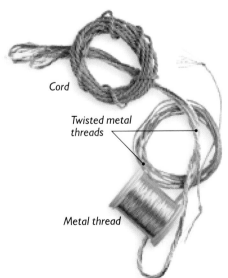

Cord

Twisted metal threads

Metal thread

STENCIL LIBRARY

All the materials you need to make the stencils are available from art and craft stores. It's best to use acetate because it lasts longer, you can see through it and it is easy to clean. Either trace the patterns, which are given actual size, directly from the book on to the acetate using a pencil, or use a photocopy. Tape the paper pattern (if applicable) and acetate on to a cutting mat to prevent it sliding around, and start cutting out the stencil, following the lines. Use a small to medium craft knife or a scalpel with a new blade. Take extra care when cutting around corners and when cutting out the more intricate parts of the design. Remove all the cuttings and you are ready to get stencilling. You can enlarge or reduce a design on a photocopying machine. When using your stencil, there is no right or wrong side. Some designs call for an image to be reversed – to do this, simply flip your stencil, having first made sure it is clean and dry.

If you're using the stencil motif as an embroidery outline, use a very sharp, hard pencil which will leave a fine line on the fabric, or an air-soluble pen, or a thin permanent marker. Water-based fabric paints are ideal for painting through the stencil. Some darken slightly as they dry.

Use stencil brushes to apply the paints. These have stiff, blunt-cut bristles and come in different sizes – the smaller the cutout, the smaller the brush should be.

The best fabrics for stencilling are smoothly woven, natural fabrics. Wash fabrics before starting to test for shrinkage and colourfastness, and to remove the finish on the fabric. Suitable fabrics include cotton, cotton mixes and linen.

YOU WILL NEED

* Acetate, cutting mat, craft knife or scalpel
* Fabric, washed and ironed
* Fabric paints, including white
* Stencil brushes
* Sharp, hard (H) pencil
* Masking tape
* Lining paper
* Spatula for mixing paints (optional)
* Old white saucer
* Paper towels

Outlining a stencil design

Lay the fabric out on a flat surface and secure it with strips of masking tape. Position the stencil and hold it firmly in place with masking tape. Using a sharp H pencil, draw round the inner edges of the cutout area, keeping the line as light and fine as possible. Alternatively, use an air-soluble pen – the marks will disappear in a few days.

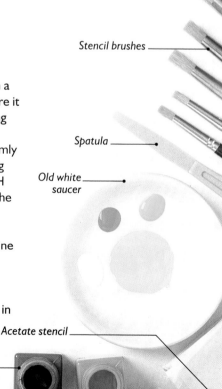

Stencil brushes

Spatula

Old white saucer

Acetate stencil

Fabric paints

Masking tape

Using the Stencils

Before you start, wash the fabric to remove any manufacturer's finishes. Cover the work surface with scrap paper or lining paper to prevent the paint staining it, then stretch the fabric taut before starting to stencil it.

Using the stencil

Stencil all the cutouts in the first colour before applying the second colour. Clean and dry the stencil and brush before applying each new colour. To avoid smudging the paint, lift the stencil off the fabric rather than sliding it off.

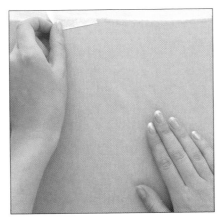

1 Cover the work surface with lining paper. Lay the fabric over the paper and smooth it out. Hold the fabric taut with strips of masking tape.

2 Use masking tape to cover all the cutout areas on the stencil you don't need for the first colour. Tape the stencil firmly in place.

3 Dip your brush in the paint and work it on the saucer until it is quite dry – avoid loading too much paint on the brush.

4 Using a firm up and down movement, dab the first colour through the cutout, starting at the outer edges and working inwards.

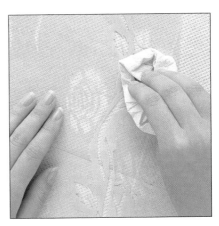

5 Remove the stencil and take off the masking tape. Clean and dry the stencil with water and a paper towel. If the paint is difficult to remove, scrub it gently with an old toothbrush.

Untidy outlines
Paint can seep under the edges of the stencil, blurring the outlines if the paint is too wet or there is too much paint on the brush. To avoid this, make sure the brush is fairly dry before you apply the colour.

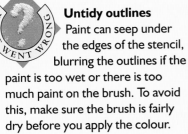
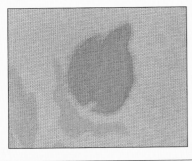

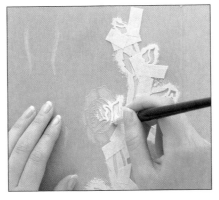

6 If any cutouts you *don't* need for the second colour butt up close to the second colour cutouts, mask them out. Leave a few areas unmasked to help you reposition the stencil, then apply the second colour as before.

7 Allow the paint to dry thoroughly. To set the colour, place a piece of kitchen paper on the paint and press it with a hot iron, according to the instructions provided by the fabric paint manufacturer.

Using Fabric Paints

Depending on how you apply the paint through the stencil — dry-brushing, stippling or sponging — you can create three completely different finishes to suit a range of embroidery stitches.

Dry brushing For a light, streaky finish which adds texture to areas which will remain unstitched, apply the paint with dry brushing.

Stippling For a background of solid colour, suitable for filling stitches such as satin stitch, use a brush to stipple on the paint.

Sponging For a speckled finish, suitable for a wide variety of stitches, apply paint with a sponge.

Materials
Brushes and sponges For dry brush and stippling, use a good quality stencil brush. For sponging, natural sponges are best. They are expensive, but you will only need a small one.

Paint palettes Art and craft shops sell ceramic and plastic palettes for mixing the paints on. Some old white saucers or small bowls cost less and will do the job just as well. Using an old brush, a flexible plastic palette knife, or a small wooden stick to mix the paints, will help avoid damaging your stencil brush, or clogging it with paint. Old teaspoons are useful for dishing out the paints from the jars.

Testing the colour
Getting the colour of the paint right is very important. The steps on page 73 explain how to do simple colour mixing, and how different fabric colours affect the paint colour. You should always test your colours and practise your techniques before starting to stencil. Use a piece of the same fabric for testing the paint colours.

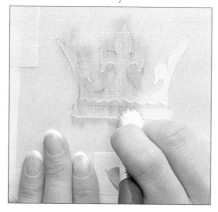

Stippling the paint gives even coverage.

Dry brushing gives a lighter effect.

Sponging the paint gives a speckled finish.

Applying paint through a stencil

Stippling Use a stencil brush to apply the paint with a firm up and down movement. The paint should sink into the fabric, rather than simply coating the surface.

Dry brushing Dip the tip of the stencil brush into the paint, and dab off the excess on kitchen paper until the brush is nearly dry. Stroke it across the cutout to create a light film of colour.

Sponging Dip the sponge in the paint and squeeze it almost dry. Dab off any excess paint on a scrap of paper, then dab the paint lightly through the stencil cutout.

Making a pastel colour

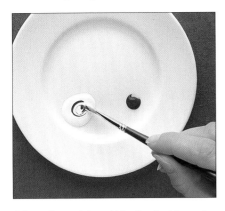

1 Put about 1 tbsp (15ml) of white paint on the saucer. Swirl in a tiny dab of the main colour.

2 Mix the colours with a small brush or a flexible palette knife, then test the colour on a spare piece of fabric.

3 Dry the paint with a hairdryer before checking the colour – the paint darkens as it dries. Add more white or coloured paint, as necessary.

Making a dark colour lighter

1 Put about 1 tbsp (15ml) of the main colour on the saucer, and add in a tiny dab of white paint.

2 Mix the paint, then test the colour on a spare piece of fabric. Dry the paint as shown above.

Fabric paint colours can look very different depending on the amount of white you mix in. The fabric strips below show four different colours, each mixed with progressively larger amounts of white.

Vermilion lightens to pink.

Gold yellow has rich creamy undertones.

Deep brown mixed with white becomes lilac.

Choosing the right colour

Always test the paint colour on your fabric before starting to stencil, as the fabric colour can alter the paint colour. Colours are truest on white (above right). On mauve, for example (below right), the same colours look drab. For clearer paint colours on coloured fabrics, add a little white to the paint.

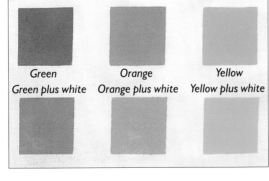

Green
Green plus white

Orange
Orange plus white

Yellow
Yellow plus white

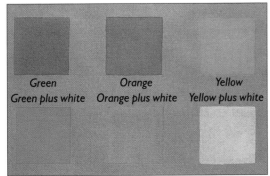

Green
Green plus white

Orange
Orange plus white

Yellow
Yellow plus white

Turquoise blue loses its strong green tones, reducing to a delicate shade of aqua.

TEMPLATES

Goldfish
pages 43-46

Crowns and Coronets
pages 21-24

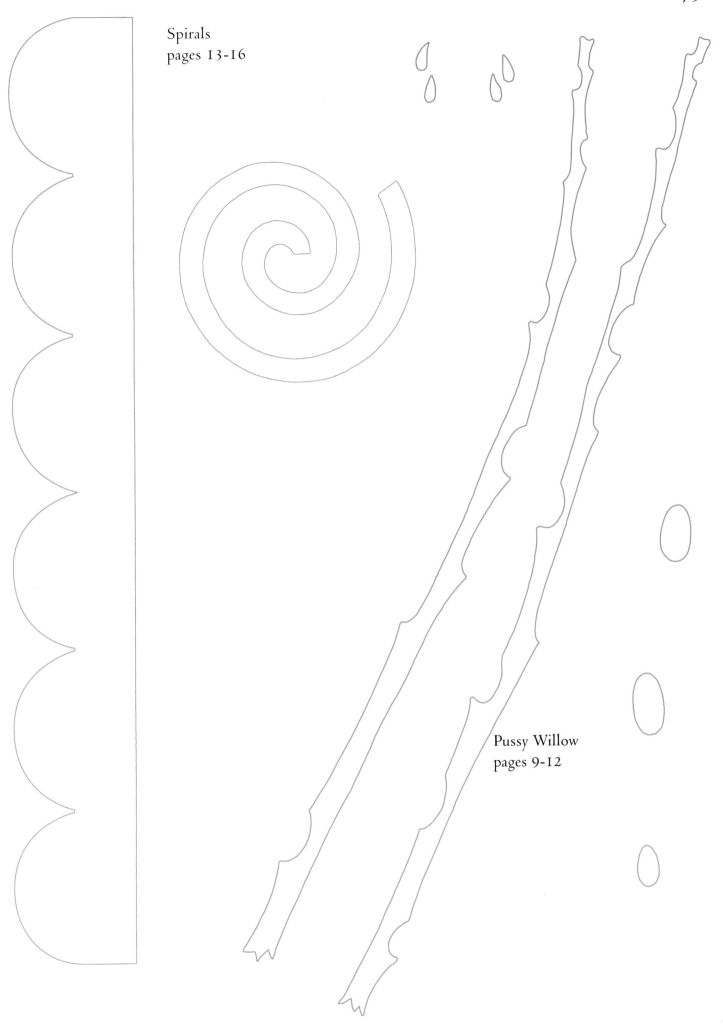

Spirals
pages 13-16

Pussy Willow
pages 9-12

Bright Hearts
pages 29-32

Chairs
pages 5-8

Geometric Blocks
pages 17-20

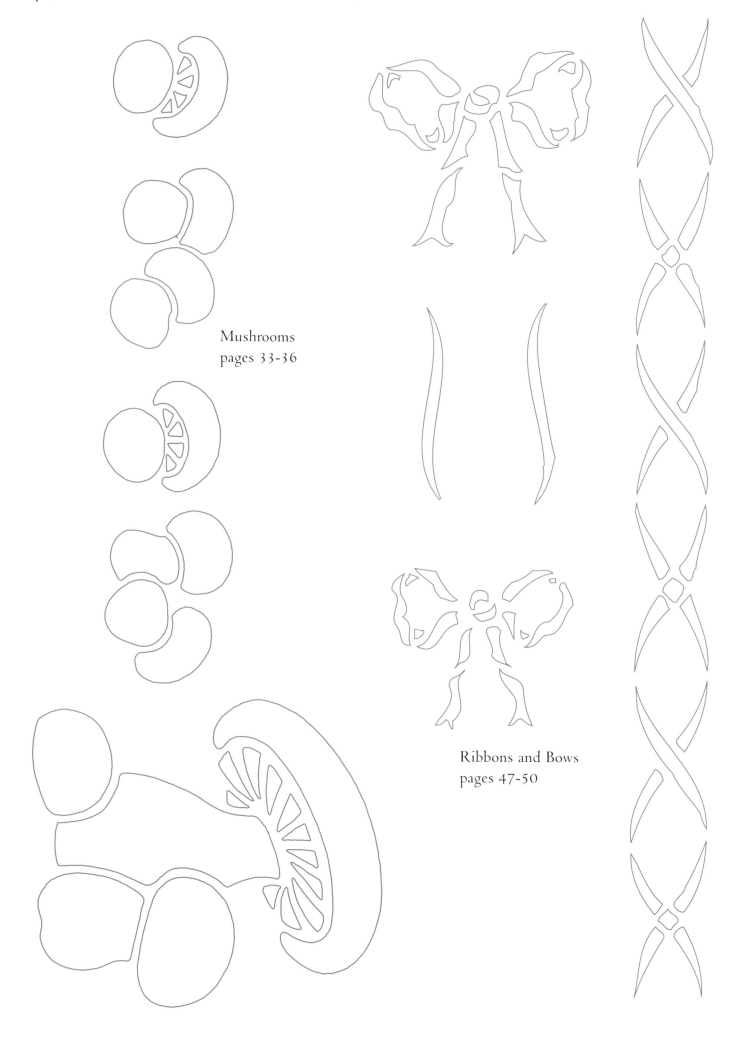

Mushrooms
pages 33-36

Ribbons and Bows
pages 47-50

Daisies
pages 51-54

Pansies
pages 25-28

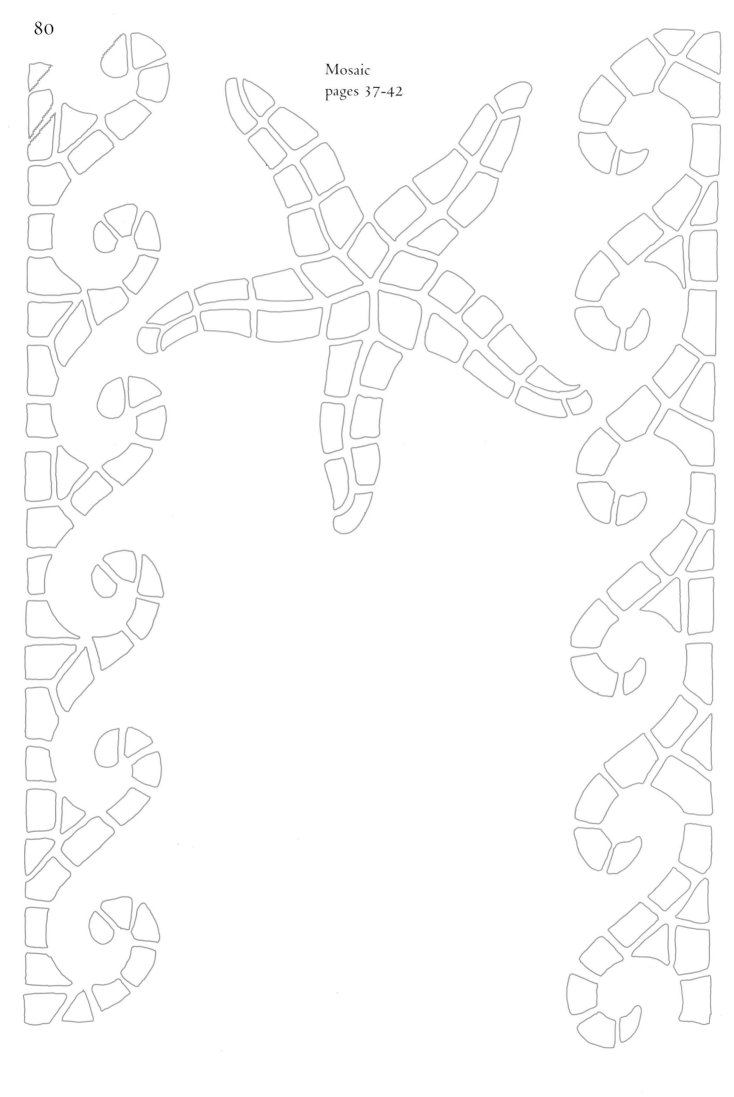

Mosaic
pages 37-42